Good people get mad…and then feel bad. It is one of life's dilemmas – why do I get so angry when I do not mean to do so. Is there a cogent and Biblical answer? Dr. Ray Burwick in this fine book takes the problem head on…and gives answers that will help all of us.

Dr. John Vawter,
Director, You're Not Alone, Inc., author, former pastor and seminary president

A must read! A masterpiece forged and refined on the anvil of years of experiences. It is a real eye opener into the raw emotion of anger that we all share with practical handles that defuse the bomb.

Dr. Dale Galloway
Dean, Beeson Institute for Advanced Church Leadership

If you are married, have children, family, and friends then you know anger happens and how it affects all relationships. This book is an excellent resource in dealing with anger and helping others deal with anger so you can resolve any conflicts that arise. The practical and biblical principles he shares will help everyone dealing with any type of anger.

Dennis Rainey
President, FamilyLife

Anger is complex. Its sources, expressions, and outcomes only add to the complexity. Ray Burwick explores this complexity in great detail, and the reader who wrestles with the insights gained from this exploration will undoubtedly benefit in many ways. In fact, the insights Burwick provides may coax and inspire us all to live more fully and to be truly good - even when we're angry!

Dr. Thomas Jay Oord
Theology Professor, Northwest Nazarene University

Freedom in Christ requires that I face squarely and honestly the issue of anger in my life. This excellent treatment of the reality of anger is a source of practical information and genuine hope. The Holy Spirit is available to guide us through the emotional maze to glorious freedom. Dr. Ray Burwick shares great insight from warm heart.

Kent Conrad
Pastor, Nampa First Church of the Nazarene

TO
My first wife, Ann, now enjoying Heaven's literal presence
with The Father
My mother, now enjoying God's and Ann's company
My children Amy, Gretchen and Ray II
Theresa, my wife since the year 2000
The multitude of clients who have taught me much
about the dynamics of anger
The many authors from whom I have garnered
gold nuggets of insight
My Lord and Savior Jesus Christ who empowers me to
conquer unhealthy anger
I AM GRATEFUL

Contents

An updated version of
<u>The Menace Within: Hurt or Anger</u> – Naphtali Books
and
<u>Anger: Defusing the Bomb</u> – Tyndale Publishers

Part One
The Hidden Killer

*How much more grievous are the consequences
of anger than the causes of it.* (Marcus Aurelius)

"You've saved me thousands of dollars and months of pain," a well-groomed middle aged woman exclaimed to me.

"Tell me about it," I responded.

She stated, "In your anger workshop last month, you suggested that hurt and anger were different feelings, but had the same root. As I began to peel off the layers of hurt, I saw a great amount of anger.

Less Anger, Less Pain.

I followed your suggestions and my pain is gone."

Nancy went on to reveal the scores of hours spent in medical examining procedures, seeking the source for undefined pain. Large amounts of money had been spent with no success. After a month of intense counseling work in anger resolution, she was experiencing physical relief.

In the following material, **"anger" will be a catchall word** that covers the gamut of related feelings - from slight annoyance to a raging hatred. It is a common theme in the Bible, appearing in **750 verses.** Use Google search engine on the Internet for "anger resolution" and in .39 of a second, you will have access to over **4,850,000 web sites** on the subject.

Everyone has "it." But not everyone realizes the devastation of unresolved anger. It is not the cause of all personal and relational problems. As you read this material, you may begin to wonder if dandruff or hair loss might not be linked to pent-up anger. (It might be.)

Anger, a leading killer

I am the first to admit there are definitely other causes for mental, emotional, physical, social and spiritual dysfunction. However, from my counseling experience and that of other counselors, unresolved anger causes these conflicts more than any other single factor. **Unresolved anger is the leading killer of happiness, health, joy, and loving relationships.** As I observe clients resolve their resentments, I see them become free to be whole and happy. Less illness. Less depression.

<table><tr><td>

Life beyond anger "management"

</td><td>

This book is written mainly for people who want to **include the spiritual dimension in their personal growth.** Many people are turned off to the church and religion, but I find very few true

</td></tr></table>

atheists. God can not only give us insights into our angry natures, but can give us the power to change what we, in our own strength, can't change about ourselves. And, **we're not just talking of controlling anger.** Anger management, as it is called in therapeutic circles, has merit and will be discussed later; but we're saying

"let's go beyond anger management and get to roots. Resolve causal factors so that there is less unhealthy anger to manage."

"Holy anger" will also be discussed and its virtues explored. **Healthy anger** along with viewing **anger as a gift** for deeper learning of oneself will also be examined.

I trust that this material will bring to us a deeper sense of freedom so we may experience all that our Creator has in mind for us.

As I reflect back to my **quarter of a century counseling people** from all walks of life, I am so grateful to have had a part in seeing people become free from emotionally-related bondage. However, not every client responded positively.

- Some left the office convinced that circumstances must dictate how they react. "**If _he_ will change, then I will be okay,**" some of them say. Their lives continue to be torn and tossed about by the pain as they hang onto that condition for recovery.
- Others left the office with a commitment to accept person-

al responsibility. They said to themselves, "Sure, I've been wronged. It hurts. I'm very resentful because of it. But I can change. I can grow through it. I can become a better person because of it."

Like a flower, the blossom opens and a deep beauty emerges from the previous hard shell of hurt and resentment. They are free -

> Blossom opens, deep beauty emerges

free to experience an abundant lifestyle not determined by circumstances.

I sincerely wish this kind of freedom for everyone who reads these pages.

Some stories are used by permission. In others, names or circumstances have been changed to insure confidentiality.

One
The Many Faces of Anger

The size of a person is measured by what makes him angry.

"Duke's trial in four deaths to begin" screamed the newspaper heading. "The 17 year-old faces four counts of capital murder and the prospect of death in the electric chair."

He had shot his father in the head and stabbed him many times. He also ended the lives of two girls, ages six and seven, and their mother.

Reason? "**Duke was angry because his father wouldn't let him drive his pickup truck.**"

A tall, fifteen-year-old boy, well mannered but shy, stood in front of his grandmother and calmly shot her to death. He was quoted as saying, "**I just wondered how it would feel to shoot grandma.**" He also shot his grandfather. Was incarcerated. Set free after 6 years.

Three years later, he confessed that during a year-long reign of terror he had murdered and dismembered six young girls in the San Francisco Bay Area, had slain his mother and strangled one of her friends.

A kindly silver-haired gentleman of **78 years of age** sat in my counseling office and said, "Ray, I've put up with my wife's criticism all these years and I just can't take it any longer. **I want a divorce.**"

"Dr. Burwick, can you tell me why I have these **chest pains**? I've been thoroughly checked out medically. Physicians can't find an organic cause for the pain. They say it is caused by tension. Can you help me?" another patient asked.

Other counselors may have different experiences, but it is **some form of anger that brings more people to my counseling office than any other factor.** As in the four cases mentioned, most of them did not realize their anger had the potential for lethal destruction. Much of anger is unrecognized.

Explosive anger is "harmful to your health." However, **hidden or unrecognized anger is by far the most devastating ire**, causing most destructive symptoms physically, emotionally, mentally, spiritually and relationally, (delineated in chapter four.)

The Swiss psychiatrist Paul Tournier addressed hidden anger when he said,

> "Violence is in the heart of all men,
> but we all have an inbuilt resistance
> to recognizing it as a thing that concerns us."

Every person may consider asking her/himself: "Does this apply to me? Can I see anger in myself? Am I an angry person and not even realize it?"

ANGER DEFINED

Anger has been defined in many ways.

- Anger is an **emotional response** to a perceived wrong or injustice. As with other emotions, physiological and biological changes result. (Increase is seen in blood pressure, adrenaline, heart rate and other biochemical responses.)
- Anger is a **signal to defend** oneself, alerting us to the invasion or potential invasion of our boundaries.
- Anger indicates a **blocked goal**.
- Anger is the impulsive response to the experience of **being deprived**. (Nouwen)
- Anger is an emotional response to **unfulfilled expectations**.
- The American Century Dictionary defines anger simply as: **"extreme or passionate displeasure."**

6

- Anger has also been described as a **"brief lunacy."**
- **Anger** is a feeling. **Aggression** is a behavior. **Violence** is the bitter effect of aggression. **Hostility** is anger with vengeance.

Anger Delineated

As I reflect on my personal and professional experiences with anger, it seems that there are three kinds of anger, all needing a unique definition.

1. The anger that God displayed in the Old Testament and the anger of Christ in the New Testament. Call it "holy anger."
2. A healthy and appropriate anger of humans.
3. An unhealthy anger.

1. GOD'S (HOLY) ANGER

God's anger is depicted many places in Scripture. Some are listed here.

> God became angry when the Israelites were **sexually immoral** with Moabite women.
>> Twenty-four thousand people died as a result (Numbers 25:1-9).
> God was angry with His people when they disobeyed and **worshipped idols**
>> (Isaiah 9:19-21 and scores of other sources.)
> God was angry when the ungrateful Israelites **complained and murmured** in the wilderness (Numbers 11:1-33).
> God was angry with those **who oppose His people** (Exodus 15:4-10.)
>> Many other situations are too numerous to mention here; but, Romans 2:5-8 probably best encapsulates God's anger.

*"But because of your **stubbornness and your unrepentant heart**,*
you are storing up wrath against yourself for the day of God's wrath,
when his righteous judgment will be revealed. God

'will give to each person according to what he has done.'
To those who by persistence in doing good seek glory, honor
and immortality, he will give eternal life.
But for those who are self-seeking and who reject the truth
and follow evil, there will be wrath and anger."

"God's wrath is an expression of His holy love. **If God is not a God of wrath, His love is no more than frail, worthless sentimentality;** the concept of mercy is meaningless; and the Cross was a cruel and unnecessary experience for His Son."[1]

For a non-theologian as myself to discuss the ramifications of God's anger is a bit ludicrous. Needless to say, we humans can't jus- tify our anger outbursts because "God got angry." **His anger was against his childrens' stubbornness and unrepentant heart and had a strong component of discipline arising from His holiness which cannot tolerate sin. It is always directed to the solution of a problem, either by correction or judgment.**

| Measure |
| your |
| anger |

(Measure your anger by that standard!)

Could God's holy anger be comparable to a daddy saying to his child who had just run out into the street without looking for approaching cars? "Because you disobeyed me, I must cause you some pain to help you remember not to run out into the street and receive the ultimate pain of getting hit by a car." A spanking fol- lows.

This is obviously a simplistic observation of God's anger, but this is not a theology book. Let's leave the definition of His anger as **that against His children who are stubborn and unre- pentant, designed to bring repentance.**

Christ's anger had a more clear-cut pattern. All the New Testament scriptures indicating His anger had at its source, **reli- gious people who were hypocrites.** One exception was his annoy-

[1]Youngblood, Ronald F., General Editor; F.F. Bruce and R.K. Harrison, Consulting Editors, *Nelson's New Illustrated Bible Dictionary*, (Nashville, TN: Thomas Nelson) 1997, c1995.

ance with the disciples for discouraging parents to bring their children to Him. Christ's anger was not selfish, (wanting His own way,) which is the common root for most of our anger.

One of my clients in justifying her anger toward her neglecting husband said, "My anger is a holy anger. It is directed to the sin of my husband who is a deacon in the church. He is a hypocrite. He talks big in church, but never talks to me. He knows so little about me that **if I died, he wouldn't be able to identify the body.**"

Molly definitely had a point. Fred was wrong in neglecting his wife. But when the fig leaves were removed, the naked truth was that Molly was mad because she wasn't getting her way. Fred wasn't treating her the way she desired.

Corrective steps were taken by both Molly and Fred. Molly repented of the sin of selfishness manifested by an angry spirit. Fred repented of his sin of selfishness demonstrated by neglecting his wife.

2. HUMAN (HOLY) ANGER

The closest we can come to experiencing God-type anger is that demonstrated by **Moses**. He was angry at the Pharaoh for not letting the Israelites free from bondage. (Exodus 11) Moses was also angry at the Israelites when they worshipped a golden calf. That anger resulted in the breaking of the commandment tablets. (Exodus 32) Notice, this was not a selfishness induced anger.

Paul demonstrated a holy anger when Elymas, the sorcerer, tried to interfere with Paul's message of Christ to Sergius Paulus. Acts 13:9-11:

Then Saul, who was also called Paul, filled with the Holy Spirit, looked straight at Elymas and said, "You are a child of the devil and an enemy of everything that is right! You are full of all kinds of deceit and trickery. Will you never stop perverting the right ways of the Lord? Now the hand of the Lord is against you. You are going to be blind, and for a time you will be unable to see the light of the sun."

Rare is our anger "holy" like that of Moses or Paul. I recall one of the few times my anger could be labeled "holy."

My young son and I were walking in a mall where one of the shops displayed a poster of a scantily clad female. It was definitely a testestorone

teaser. I felt I could handle it with a disciplined mind, but to throw a youngster into that **pictorial slime-pit** was unfair to him and to other children seeing the poster. I walked into the store, explained my position to the store manager and he invited me to leave, saying, "That is one of our best money makers. I'm not taking it down."

The anger propelled me to the mall manager where I calmly explained my concerns. The following day, the poster was gone. **Holy anger expressed brought positive results.** (That was a rare experience for me. Usually my anger is described in the next section - unhealthy anger.)

A holy anger to abortion doctors has resulted in the beginnings of many homes for unwed mothers. Of course, there is holy anger gone awry, where abortion doctors have been murdered.

The Godhead demonstrated a holy anger to which we can emulate. Move with me to the next category.

3. UNHEALTHY ANGER

Unhealthy anger is the type of anger that we experience most of the time. I will define it simply as **"the emotional energy we experience when we don't get our way."** Some don't like the bluntness of that definition and sophisticate it a bit by saying "the energy we experience when an obstacle is confronted in the process of need-fulfillment - a blocked goal." That sounds so much more adult. However, we're less inclined to rid ourselves of unhealthy anger if we don't see the selfishness and destructiveness in the attitudes underlying the anger. 'Blocked goal" doesn't provide us with sufficient motivation to remedy unhealthy anger.

Most of our anger is based in selfishness and when we peel back the protective layers of our selfishness, we find a level of anger toward God for His failure to provide for us what we want.

10

> **Unhealthy anger is never just human-directed**
> **but is also an assault on God's sovereign care of us.**

The Bible has examples of unhealthy anger: God accepted Abel's offering, not Cain's. Result? **Cain** - jealous and angry, murdered his brother. **Esau** carelessly gave his birthright to Jacob, his brother. He became angry and plotted Jacob's death.

As with Cain and Esau, unhealthy anger often plays out as a person's condemning judgment, a usurpation of God's role as judge.

4. HEALTHY ANGER

There is an anger that would be classified neither holy not unhealthy. **Healthy anger is an appropriate anger response toward a source of abuse.**

So frequently in the counseling office I encounter a client who is therapeutically stuck. Usually trapped in a depression or in a destructive compulsive behavior. Invariably, freedom came when the client allowed herself to face and resolve the rage within from being sexually abused. **Sexual abuse anger is so frequently buried.**

Obscuring thought processes that help bury the anger sound like this: "It wasn't that bad." "It didn't really happen." "It was my fault." "But he was my dad. I love him."

The hurt, the pain, the anger is buried (repressed). For personal growth, for release from the bondage, healthy and appropriate anger directed toward the abuser must be faced and expressed in some healthy manner. The process will be explained later in the book.

A dear friend of mine was **sexually abused** at the age of 12 at a summer camp. His story: "I felt a little guilty because **I enjoyed the physical pleasure and the attention** the camp counselor gave me. My dad was not an affectionate man. Didn't even know he loved me. This counselor reached out to me, took the initiative to express what I thought was love to me. For years I didn't realize the negative effects on my sexual relationship with my wife. At the age of 55, I finally put it all together and became very angry at the camp counselor.

> "The <u>awareness</u> of how that experience was effecting my current sexual relationship with my wife. The <u>release</u> of that anger and the subsequent <u>forgiving</u> that took place, resulted in a freeing of sexual conflict in my marriage."

Though a controversial figure and one with whom some would disagree frequently, the consumer activist Ralph Nader, has saved countless lives because his anger led him to challenge the apathy of the industrial community to safety and quality. Healthy anger. It has been said that the world needs anger. The world often continues to allow evil because it isn't angry enough.

Holy anger. Healthy anger. Unhealthy anger. Got any? Let's learn more about the dynamics of anger in the next chapter.

<u>Chapter exercise:</u>

1. Sometimes we are not aware of our anger and its destructiveness. Examining the following words could put you in touch with unrecognized anger. Do you relate to any of the following "anger" words? **Circle any that apply**.

annoyed, displeased, disgusted, frustrated, offended, resentful, impatient, cross, irate, livid, infuriated, crabby, exercised, bitter, rage, inner turmoil, furious, sullen, pouting, irritable, hurt, devastated, ticked/teed off, mad, griped, fed up, sore, hot-under-the-collar, seething, annoyed, troubled, furious, inflamed, indignant, antagonistic, exasperated, vexed, provoked, irked, sick, pained, hostile, ferocious, vicious, deadly, dangerous

2. List situations that have demonstrated your healthy anger.

3. List holy anger situations experienced.

4. In what situations have you most recently experienced unhealthy anger?

Scripture:
I Timothy 2:8 *I want men everywhere to lift up holy hands in prayer, without anger or disputing.*

Prayer:
   Father, I desire to be an effective communicator with you - one who can pray effectively. If there is any <u>healthy</u> or <u>unhealthy</u> anger residing within me, please show it to me. Help me see if there is any holy anger that needs constructive expression.

Two
The Devil Made Me Do It

Sources of Anger

Anger is a thief who steals away nice moments. (Lunden)

"**Why do I get so angry?**" some people ask the counselor. Others say: "I've tried so hard to control my anger. It seems impossible." Some report: "I didn't realize I was such an angry person until I had that explosive reaction to my wife."

What are the sources of anger - especially unhealthy anger?

☛ **We are born angry.**

Sigmund Freud, the father of modern psychology, the perpetrator of some strange ideologies, had no conflict with the Bible when he said: "Man is born basically evil."

> *"We started out bad,*
> > *being born with evil natures,*
> > > *and were under God's anger..."*
> > > > the Living Bible tells us in Ephesians 2:3.

Evidence indicates that some infants are born more irritable and easily angered than others. They seem to have a low tolerance for frustration and as they grow older, seem to feel they don't deserve inconvenience or annoyance.

Many years ago, when I was disciplining one of our children for disobedience, she said, "**Daddy, if Adam hadn't sinned, I wouldn't be in trouble now!**" Adam and Eve started the disobedience and rebellion, but we all follow on que!

I don't deserve to be inconvenienced!

We realize that our children have to be taught wholesome attitudes and behavior, and, as they obey God, He makes them "good." We don't have to teach them to be "bad." That comes characteristically.

☞ Anger develops naturally

We see the origins of anger clearly when observing a baby when it doesn't get its way. One of our friends has an infant son who doesn't like to lie on his stomach. When his father places him in that position, the crib becomes bedlam. The baby kicks and squirms, his face gets red, and he becomes furious because he cannot get over onto his back.

Such behavior is normal and appropriate for a child, but

> **childish temper tantrums often evolve into adults'
> sophisticated anger, which frequently displays
> itself in self-pity and depression.**

☞ Anger is learned

> *Keep away from angry, short-tempered men*
> <u>*lest you learn to be like them*</u> *and endanger your soul.*
> (Proverbs 22:24-25 TLB).

> It has been said, **"We become like the books we read
> and the people with whom we associate."**

When an angry teenager comes to my counseling office, invariably, at least one of the parents was also a very angry person. **Since the parent's anger wasn't resolved, it was being modeled to, and learned by the children.**

Do children have the right to say to their parents, "I'm angry because I'm just like you?"

Even so, the child must mature to the point that he accepts personal responsibility to "unlearn" the poor ways of expressing anger: neither acting it out or turning it destructively inward.

> *That which is learned,*
> *can be unlearned and*
> *healthy patterns relearned.*

☞ **Self esteem affects anger**

Poor self esteem leads to self-absorption, a greater awareness of self. The more self absorbed, the greater our needs appear to be and the greater the awareness of how circumstances affect us.

> **Self-esteem induced anger**

For one with poor self esteem, if things don't go his way, he becomes fearful and threatened, perhaps even envious or hurt, all of which lead directly to anger.

My parenting is a prime example of this. I felt very insecure as a father and as a leader of the home. I felt I had to have control of everything. If a child (or my wife) questioned my decision, or didn't follow my lead, I became threatened and angry. Though desiring to be a godly man, **my godliness hadn't penetrated my insecurity.** There were times, sad to say, that I was not a pleasant fixture in the home!

> **Parental Insecurity**

Stu Weber describes insecurity-related-anger well in his book Spirit Warriors. "Keep in mind that **angry intimidation** has been a stock-in-trade **military motivator** for centuries. As a young officer, I'd seen leaders blowing their stacks all the time. I thought that was just how it was done. It always seemed to pick up the pace of whatever task was at hand. I was even beginning to use it with my own men now and then.

"But my brigade commander, 'the old man,' told me something that went completely against the grain. He said, '**There is a place for anger, but it is rare.** Commonplace, angry displays of temper are more often than not actually a **substitute for a lack of leadership skills on the part of an insecure leader.**'"

17

Feelings of inadequacy, insecurity, poor self esteem contribute to an anger problem.

☞ Fear

You don't have to be insecure to be fearful. Just being out of control of a situation can raise the hackles of fear. Have you ever waited for a loved one to get home? He is late. Thirty minutes tardy creates some fear. "Is he okay?. Has he had a wreck?" Sixty minutes heightens the fear. Notice how anger is rearing its head. In this case, anger is a result of fear. Out of control.

Or, as with my children, anger at Dad because of fear of being controlled by him.

☞ Manipulative anger

Somewhat tied to the self esteem issue are those who, not feeling strong within themselves, display anger to manipulate others to get their way.

I recall one client. He stood about six foot four, weighed nearly 300 pounds. He had a blustering demeanor that tended to make people afraid of him. When his wife would have a suggestion for

> Family War on Terror

the family that he didn't like, he would just raise his voice. **His size and voice reduced his wife** to a **position of passive doormat**. He always got his way. His children learned the technique well and poor mama got it from all directions... until she got tired of eating carpet.

Through counseling, prayer and practice, she became a stronger woman, stood up to her family appropriately and all hell broke loose. For a few weeks it was not a pretty sight. It was like a **family war on terror until boundaries were established and angry manipulation bombed**. Peace was restored when dad and children realized their angry manipulative behavior had no payoff.

☞ Guilt covering

Another source of anger is a denial of guilt. Or possibly, not wanting to resolve a guilt issue.

Janice was having an affair. Being brought up in the church, her moral training was definitely revealing guilt. Joe felt something was amiss, couldn't put a finger on it but tried to discuss it with Janice. **Her anger diverted hers and Joe's attention away from the real issue** - her guilty behavior. He was a peace-keeper, so Janice's anger would shut him up.

The story didn't end well. She left the church. Left Joe and her children. Broken hearts. Broken family. Guilty behavior was not rectified. Janice was unrepentant and began a new life. But that was not the end of the tale. Her adultery ended when her lover realized he didn't want the responsibility of marriage. **Janice lost her family, her church, peace of mind and her lover**.

Anger, that camouflaged guilt, was her focus.   End result: destruction.

☞ Volcanic anger

Another source of anger is a **build-up of anger** that can get hooked into and come out explosive. Usually people with a "bad temper" are those who have not resolved anger in their lives and it continues to build up the same way lava builds within a volcano. A **current situation reminds them of a previous "abuse"** that for some reason was too difficult or was unable to be resolved. The present anger is intensified by the past unresolved anger.

> Past unresolved anger intensifies present anger.

The combination can be a <u>lethal redirection</u> of all the anger to the current source.

James is an example. Being raised in a very legalistic church, he was taught that good Christians didn't get angry. He bottled his. A controlling, overbearing mother was the source of his tremendous pent up rage that didn't explode until he got married. He knew his fiancé, Lisa, as a passive girl who didn't make waves. He didn't realize that there were unresolved issues in her from childhood. <u>Wife Lisa</u> was not the same as <u>fiancé Lisa</u>. Sparks began flying when

Lisa would not go along with some of James's ideas. The volcano blew a couple weeks after the wedding. "You are as controlling as my mother," shouted James. "I'm not going to be married to my mother. **If it weren't for you, I could be a good Christian.**"

The shock of his explosion rocked both of them. A counselor was sought. The volcano was explored and diffused. Lisa also had to face abuse issues from her dad that were being displaced on James.

The <u>other cause for volcanic anger explosions</u> is **current stress**. This can be <u>internal</u> stress, like premenstrual tension or <u>external</u> pressure of a tense situation. If one tends to be an angry person, prevailing stress reveals more clearly what lies within. **The angry spirit is more observable.**

Thus, if a person recognizes a tendency toward temper outbursts (or anger implosions where the body suffers from internalized anger), two questions can be asked.

- Have I considerable unresolved anger from the past that needs correction?
- Am I not handling current stress well and it is revealing an angry spirit within?

Roots for all of our unhealthy anger:
- <u>Learned behavior,</u>
- <u>self esteem issues,</u>
- <u>fear,</u>
- <u>manipulative anger,</u>
- <u>guilt camouflage,</u>
- <u>emotional volcanoes</u>
- <u>self-centeredness</u>.

Some psychological theories differ with these views of anger by adhering to a medical model believing that anger is a **biological phenomenon** built into the gene structure. According to this view, **aggression must be released through culturally acceptable outlets and treated with medication**. And, there are medications that reduce the intensity of anger. However, in my opinion, they just mask emotional issues that lie unresolved and the person "lives better chemically,"- for a while!

Look with me at the **next chapter's portrayal of anger distortions**.

Exercise:

We all get angry. Did you gain any insights into the source(s) of your anger? Sometimes those close to us recognize things about us we don't see. It might be helpful to **go over this material with a close friend or spouse and ask them what they see in you.**

1. Which of the listed anger sources best describe you?
   **Selfishness.   Learned anger.   Fragile self esteem.
   Fear. Manipulation.   Guilt covering.   Volcanic anger.**

2. Do you relate to any of the following verbs depicting **actions motivated by anger?**
   Consider circling those that apply to you.

To: hate,   wound,   damage,   annihilate,   despise,   scorn, disdain,   loathe,   vilify,   curse,   ruin,   demolish,   abhor, abominate,   ridicule,   tease,   get even,   laugh at,   humiliate, goad,   shame,   criticize,   cut down,   take out,   spite on, rail at,   scold,   bawl out,   irritate,   beat up,   ostracize, fight,   beat, vanquish,   crush,   brutalize,   offend,   bully

Scripture:

James 3:13-16 *Who is wise and understanding among you? Let him show it by his good life, by deeds done in the humility that comes from wisdom. But if you __harbor bitter envy__ and__ selfish ambition__ in your hearts, do not boast about it or deny the truth. Such "wisdom"* *does not come down from heaven but is <u>earthly, unspiritual, of the</u>* <u>*devil*</u>*. For where you have envy and selfish ambition, there you find disorder and every evil practice.*

Prayer:

Father, it is not my desire to blame anyone else for my anger. I take full responsibility for it. However, there may be a source that I haven't seen before that is leading me to point the finger with malice. Help me blame that person just long enough to fully feel and own the anger and its source and then take full responsibility for processing it in a healthy way.

Three
What's Behind The Mask

Distorted Anger Processing
'When angry count to four; when very angry, swear."
(Mark Twain)

Distorted Expressions of Anger

Buried Anger

"I never get angry," he said. Robert, a meticulously dressed middle-aged man sat in my office, facing not only a possible divorce but the criminal charge of attempted murder.

"What do you mean?" I asked. "everyone gets angry at times."

"Not me," replied Robert with a taint of pride in his voice.

Robert's wife, Shirley, had been driving because Robert had become too intoxicated

> **Repression:**
> a denial of
> anger

again. Shirley had criticized him for drinking and the tank exploded - Robert's that is. He pulled a revolver out of the glove compartment and **shot at her**. Fortunately, in his drunken stupor his aim was poor - he missed.

Robert is an example of an anger distortion called **repression**, or buried anger, which is an **unconscious denial or non-admittance of anger; the stuffing of anger into the subconscious mind.**

The repressed person, who buries his anger, might say he never gets angry. Either this person is a liar, has a poor memory, lives a very dull life, is first in line for the first vacancy in the Trinity or is deceiving himself. **Anger is a natural emotion** which everyone experiences. Robert was not first in line for the first vacancy in the Trinity!

In the cases of rape with which I'm familiar, it was not sexual lust that was the prompter of the crime, but a buried resentment toward significant female figures - usually beginning with the

I'm not angry,
just teed off.

mother. **Rape was a way of gaining control of and expressing buried rage**, though in such a destructive way.

Canned Anger

Similar to buried anger is canned anger - a **suppressing** of the anger feelings. So often I hear Christians say: "Yes, sir, since I've become a Christian, I'd like to report to you that I've completely controlled my temper. I still get angry, but no one else knows about it. I keep it inside," such a person claims, often with a look of piety and a hint of self-righteousness.

> **Suppression: anger shoved down, sat on, covered over, masked.**

A person who is suppressing anger shoves it within, sits on it, covers it over, masks it, and soon my not even be aware of it.

Canned anger is often characterized by "I just put it out of my mind. I try to forget it. I take a pill or a shot of whiskey. I just laugh it off. No one is going to control me."

But the **reservoir of anger builds** and the **accumulated poison** becomes more and more potent. Canned hostility is not necessarily hostility conquered. **Hostility can be a very silent, sleeping terrorist, but the slightest provocation will bring it forth in all its ugliness.** Like the lava trapped in the Mt. St. Helen's volcano, it had to flow.

Maggie's thoughts taken from a web site are:

"Anger is a funny thing. I suppose you could say that it's my favorite weapon that I use on myself. I don't have uncontrollable outbursts of anger, I have uncontrollable 'inbursts' of anger. I get angry at myself and beat myself up before it ever reaches the surface and hurts anyone else. I'm afraid of what will happen if I 'let it fly.' **I'm afraid that I won't be a 'good girl' anymore.**

"I don't want anyone else to get hurt because of me. Even when I do get angry at other people, I hold on to it. There's a whole lot of **anger churning** around inside me, but I don't know how to get it out without hurting anyone. I know that I'm really angry about a lot of things, I just don't know what to do with all that anger. **It just sits there like a time-bomb waiting to destroy me.**"

The person who buries anger says, "I am not aware of anger," while one (like Maggie) with canned anger says, "I'm aware of anger, but I'll keep it under wraps. It'll stay within me"

Transference

Psychology calls this kind of misdirected anger, **displacement**. Sometimes we remove anger from the directed source because, for some reason, we are too threatened to admit the fact that we are angry at the boss, at our spouse, or at God. We transfer the anger to a less threatening source or situation.

> Displacement: A less threatening source receives the anger

Transference is depicted by the man who gets angry at his boss but cannot resolve it. If he spewed out anger at work, or tried to confront his boss, he might get fired. So he takes that anger home with him and transfers it to his wife with comments like, "Why isn't dinner ready? I thought we were going to have roast duck, but I see it's burnt offering!" The **wife receives the brunt of the man's transferred anger and she becomes angry**.

Transference may continue. Instead of resolving it within herself and with her husband, she then lashes out at the child. The child, not able to resolve anger because he or she does not see parents working through and resolving anger, then kicks the dog. The dog bites, the cat, and the cat goes to the backyard and chases a chipmunk. On and on we go, dumping our anger on illegitimate sources.

Transference

Pro basketball provides us with another **example of transference**. In an article written for a web site,

> "Of course, sometimes, fights come out of nowhere. A guy is at home, his wife rips him for not getting her friends enough tickets in the lower bowl, and the next thing you know, the player is throwing punches. He's angry at his wife, of course, but he is taking it out on some poor schlub just trying to get some minutes in to keep his paycheck coming for another month."

Transference does not resolve anger, but transfers it to some less threatening object – usually a person.

Camouflage

The fourth distorted expression of anger is camouflage. Though this distortion could be an example of repression, there appears to be a slight difference.

A barrier resides between thinking and feeling. Feelings are masked. Paul Tournier writes in his book <u>Violence Within</u> describing it as internal and external languages:

> "But when the gulf is widened between the internal and external languages, like the two banks of a river becoming further apart, it becomes impossible eventually to bridge the gap, and **the result is a state of anxiety, a sign of rupture in the unity of the person.** The psychotherapist's consulting room, with its exceptional climate of truth, is the place where a bridge can be built joining the two sides together again, so that the patient may at last become his real self."

It seems that the more intelligent my clients are, the more they tend to intellectualize their feelings, camouflaging their anger. For

| Camouflage: to intellectualize feelings. |

example, a brilliant young physician sat in my counseling office. His psychiatrist had told him that **electro shock treatments were the only way to bring him out of his depression.**

"Ray, there is no way I can have shock treatments. My practice would be ruined." His surgical practice and brilliant mind had been his life. A rejecting wife, some professional criticism, childhood hurts, and rejections had led Dr. Sam to a deep-seated resentment that had smoldered within him for years. It had found its outlet through depression so profound that he was **at the point of taking his life.**

As we discussed his hurts and frustrations, the doctor was quick to make comments like, "But, I love her," or "My parents did their best," or 'He couldn't help it," or "But look how bad I was in that situation."

Instead of looking at the feelings of hurt, resentment, bitterness and even hate, Sam would quickly **intellectualize the circumstances.** Feelings were not surfaced and resolved. Anger was camouflaged - even resulting in suicidal thoughts.

One of the most frequent camouflages I hear in counseling is the statement: "I was hurt." Invariably, the person who makes that statement is a very angry person, because the word

"hurt" is a blanket that often covers a bed of anger.

Hurt is often the initial stage of anger or is a complacent form of anger. Hurt and anger feel differently, but they are flip sides of the same coin. If you are only feeling "hurt" chances are great that you are not in touch with your anger.

Other phrases I hear that camouflage anger are, "I'm a Christian, so I forgive." "I'm sanctified. Sanctified people don't get angry." But all the evidence shows the person is in fact quite angry. One preacher told me, "I'm not angry. My voice is loud because I'm exercised. Only fools get angry." I wished I had a mirror to let him see how angry his "exercised" face looked!

Camouflaging anger, so destructive to mind and body.

Venting

A lashing out, explosive method of expressing anger. On a web site, Sera describes hers: "My anger sometimes isolates me, by ruining relationships with the very people that I love the most. **It keeps me from getting close to someone** when I know I really would like to know them better. It **keeps me from opening up and sharing** my real feelings. Then the anger just builds up more and more until it is finally let out, and then shocks everyone, because they never knew I felt that way.

"I have a great deal of trouble letting go of my anger. I know I need to, but it's terribly difficult to do so. I know my anger just builds up and harms me emotionally, but still I find it hard to let go of the anger and accept that I need to try and move on. I never know when it'll happen. **One moment I feel well, and the next my anger becomes overwhelming.** Hopefully, as time goes on, the anger will subside."

Venting anger in a lashing out fashion is probably healthier for the body but that method of anger expression has two downsides. Relationships are certainly battered (as Sera described); and, research indicates that

> **the more one vents anger, the stronger is the tendency to be even more angry.**

Anger buried, canned, transferred, camouflaged and vented - all distortions that lead to unhealthy relationships and unhealthy living in general. How do these twists come about? Where does anger distortion begin?

Genesis of Anger

☞ **Anger stifled**

Anger distortion has a genesis, usually in childhood when children are taught to stifle

> "Stuff it, kid."

anger. Parents often tell children not to get angry with them. Or perhaps parents tell children not to hold in anger, but have threatened them with such remarks as, "Let it out, but I will knock your block off if you are disrespectful," indicating their own disrespectful attitude.

A healthy home climate is one of openness where children are allowed to tell parents of their anger. Anger can be expressed in a very dishonoring way, and parents cannot let children do that. If a parent is attacked verbally or physically, or is called names, or if hate is expressed in a disrespectful way, a child should be firmly disciplined.

An example of an honoring expression was demonstrated by 10-year-old Jason. "Mom, I'm very angry with you. You embarrassed me in front of my friends when you asked me if I had brushed my teeth. It made me feel like a little boy that mother has to watch over. The boys laughed at me later."

Where did Jason learn this very appropriate expression of anger? He had a mother who was respectful in the way she expressed

> **Speak the truth, in love!**

her anger to her husband and her children. A very rare person, indeed. Her biblical challenge was "Speak the truth - in love." She was a magnificent model for those with whom she came in contact.

☞ **Stoic parent**

Anger distortion is also demonstrated to the child by a stoic, or non feeling parent who says, "It's crazy to get angry. What good does it do?" Anger gets buried, and the child is not taught how to express or resolve anger in a constructive manner.

Again, we should **encourage our children to express anger**

constructively and politely. The child explains his position. The parent listens and explains his viewpoint. Conflict is discussed. Whether the clash is resolved or not, anger has to be dealt with biblically, as we will discuss later.

As we mature from childhood to adulthood, hindrances thwart expressing and resolving anger.

Hindrances to expression and resolution

☞ Fear

Some of us must face the fact that if we really saw what is going on within us, we would see homicide. "Am I a monster?" we would ask ourselves. In fact, we have even allowed our feelings to surface occasionally enough to say, "I'd like to do that person physical harm!" Some of us do not like to face the monster within because of a **fear that we might actually succumb to the murderous thoughts.**

Other <u>fears</u> that stifle expression of anger:

> fear of <u>rejection</u>, of <u>hurting others</u>, of <u>being hurt</u> by others, of <u>repeating dysfunctional angry behavior</u> modeled by a parent,
> of others seeing an expression of anger as a <u>weakness</u> of ours.

☞ "Nice guy" syndrome

Nice men and women are uncomfortable with their anger. They believe an expression of anger will label them "unnice." This is probably more so with women then men. Society rewards the female who covers up her anger. "She's a nice lady." **Often women who express anger are labeled "bitchy."**

And there are some women who use anger to try to get a spouse to change when he doesn't want to change. She becomes at best a nag, at worst, "bitchy." The counterproductive behavior elicits his disapproval and disrespect. She along with the "nice lady" is left helpless and powerless.

☛ Emotional isolation

Some isolate themselves emotionally, like the person who says, "I won't get involved. I have been hurt enough." In order not to be hurt any more, such a person builds **walls around himself**. Consequently, with no emotional involvement, there is no cause for anger to flare. However,

I've been hurt enough

all the stored up hurt that takes on the form of mortar holding those bricks together, is covering a reservoir of unresolved anger.

☛ Insecurity

Others say, "<u>I must control. I must **be in control**</u> of my feelings. They won't be expressed." The opinions of others are considered so important and since people admire a controlled person, the insecure, controlled person is hindered from resolving his anger.

An angry doormat!

Insecurity is also manifested in an **inability to confront**. Often, an insecure wife who has been taught to "submit" feels like a doormat. In her passivity she becomes subservient, too insecure to confront. In her dishonesty she becomes a very angry doormat at that. Her insecurity breeds a fear of rejection. "If I tell my husband that I'm angry about what is going on, or if I tell him that he isn't fair, he might reject me. He might even leave me."

Christian men, who from the pulpit or from the Bible, <u>focus</u> on the verse, "Wives submit" are **insecure men**. They have not only been unsuccessful at processing their own anger, but also own a significant amount of fragile maleness. A man's insecurity relegates his wife to a lower position, giving him a sense of superiority - though a false one!

☛ Distorted Christianity

The last hindrance to expressing and resolving anger we'll examine is a distorted idea about Christianity. Some say, "Christians aren't supposed to get angry, so I can't be angry. It's a sin to be angry. I can't be sanctified if I'm angry. I'm not angry. I'm just upset."

> **"Christian" Denial**

I mentioned previously the minister who said to me, "Ray, I'm not angry. I'm just exercised!" He felt if he labeled his feelings "angry," he would be sinning and he could not stand the fact that there might be any sin in his life.

Exercise:

Such anger distortions and hindrances often indicate a heightened concern about ones reputation. "What would people think if they saw me angry?" For some, this insight, this recognition of themselves, helps them begin to resolve unhealthy anger properly. Others must suffer some of the emotional, physical, mental, spiritual and relational effects of anger obstacles before they are motivated to seek better solutions.

Do you see yourself?
Any distortions:
buried, canned, transferred, camouflaged or vented anger?
Any hindrances:
fear, nice guy, emotional isolation, insecurity or distorted Christianity?

Circle any of the distortions or hindrances listed above, that could typify you.

Again, a close friend or spouse can sometimes point out these things within us better then

I wasn't angry,
I was under pressure

we can see them ourselves. Do you have such
a friend who would hold up the mirror to you?

Scripture:
Proverbs 29: 25

> *Fear of man* will *prove to be a <u>snare</u>, but whoever trusts in the LORD is kept safe.*

Prayer

Father, I desire to be a godly person. I want to have a right-eous fear of You and not an unhealthy fear of man. If I'm unaware of fear-induced anger distortions or hindrances, please enlighten me so that I can be more free of emotional baggage. I desire to experience the fullness of the abundant life in You.

Four

The Hidden Killer

Destructive Results of Anger

He who angers you conquers you. (Kenny)

Anger is indeed one of the main obstacles of the spiritual life.
The longer I am here, the more I sense how anger bars my way
to God.
Henri Nouwen

Unresolved anger releases a considerable amount of biochemical poison in the body. From my counseling experience, it seems as if **unresolved anger is the underlying cause of nearly everything wrong with us.**

Obviously, I am being facetious. Fear, worry, insecurity, trauma of various types, virus, birth defects, biochemical imbalance, drug abuse - all these and more can cause disease. But as I see my clients resolving their anger issues, I observe a significant lessening of destructive symptoms, more than with any other kind of resolution. Most depression ceases, anxiety diminishes, migraines, stomach and intestinal disorders and a host of other complaints become less intense or no problem at all.

Let's look at some of the results of unresolved anger, beginning with the most devastating.

☛ Death

With psychiatrists Minirth and Meier in <u>Happiness is a Choice</u>, **I believe anger is probably the leading cause of death.** The first example of death by murder in Scripture is that of Cain killing Abel. Jealousy prompted it. (Genesis 4:5,8)

See also 1 Samuel 22:18; Exodus 2:12; Genesis 49:6,7; Matthew 2:16; Acts 7:57-60; 1 John 3:15; John 19:6

37

William James tells us:
**"Man is the most formidable beast of preyand the only
one that preys systematically on his own species,"**

Examining dynamics underlying the numerous **school killings**,
you'll find a motivation of anger. From the **terrorists** of 9-11, to the
road rage shooters, anger is an underlying issue.
One research on homicide indicated that **90 per-** | Absence of
cent of the murderers grew up with a father who | Fathers: a
was absent, brutal, alcoholic or else so passive | source of
and demeaned as to command no respect. | murder.
Definitely a source of anger-related murder.

Absence of Fathers: a source of murder.

However, death by gun or exploding an airplane into a sky-
scraper are not the major sources of casualty.

**The more subtle killer is the poison of anger
within that destroys its own container.**

A friend told me that his father was so angry he had **choked to
death**. In checking with a medical doctor about this, I was told that
anger can induce a vomiting episode that can cause aspiration
(choking).

Suicides can often be traced to a combination of depression
and anger. One client told me that a note had been found beside
her husband who had shot himself in the head, reading: **"I love my
God. I love my country. I hate my wife. She's a bitch."**

To understand the possible dynamics let's look at:

ANGER'S FREQUENT SEQUENCE

- **An expectation**, unfulfilled, leads to
- **irritation/hurt/anger**; if unresolved, leads to
- **resentment/bitterness**;if unresolved, leads to

- <u>**self-pity / depression / anxiety / fears / psychosomatic disease and distorted self image**</u>; if unresolved, leads to
- <u>**withdrawal**</u>; if unresolved, leads to
- <u>**greater self-absorption and expectations;**</u> if unresolved, leads to a life of
- <u>**chronic misery, psychotic break and even suicide.**</u>

> Could suicide be the ultimate expression of anger?

I could relate many suicide stories of clients who shared with me about the loss of a spouse or child who had been very angry with them. It has caused me to wonder if suicide is <u>often</u> the ultimate destructive expression of anger! Obviously not all suicide is anger-related. Pride drove King Saul to take his own life by sword. (1 Samuel 31:4)

John Hunter (1728-1793), an English physician, is reported to have developed angina pectoris (chest pains caused by deficient oxygenation of the heart muscles) and was one of the first to describe the symptoms. He has been quoted as saying, *"My life is in the hands of any rascal who chooses to annoy and tease me."*

Violent disagreements with his colleagues brought on the chest pains. The results of the disagreements hastened his death and a heart attack finally ended his life.

> **Women's' Death Stats**

Women who **habitually stifle high levels of anger** had a **death rate** during an 18 year study, **three times higher** than women **who release their anger**, according to a University of Michigan research project.

Unresolved, unprocessed anger can cause death.

☞ Bitterness

> "The mind can move from being <u>troubled</u>
> to <u>irritated</u> to <u>anger</u> to <u>vengefulness</u>," Henri Nouwen.

The reservoir of accumulated anger within us might be lying dormant, but very often it activates into grotesque, poisonous, bitter shapes, not recognizable as anger. When a root of bitterness springs to the surface, **it not only destroys the person within but relationships without**. It contaminates all it touches.

"See to it that no one misses the grace of God and that no bitter root grows up to cause trouble and defile many." (Hebrews 12:15).

Accumulated, dormant anger has been demonstrated as destructive by a research lab. Charlotte van Oyen Witvliet, an assistant professor of psychology at Hope College, lead a study about **memories and blood pressure**. When the 71 volunteers were told to **recall a past hurt**, tests recorded steep **spikes in blood pressure, heart rate and muscle tension**, <u>the same responses that occur when people are angry</u>. When the volunteers were challenged to imagine empathizing and even forgiving the people who had wronged them, they remained calm by comparison.

Anger can be spontaneous. <u>Bitterness is a choice</u>.

Ruth and Naomi are prime examples of folk who refused to become bitter. Besides losing her husband to death, <u>Ruth</u> lost her familiar, lifelong homeland and all that entailed, to be loyal to Naomi. Her faith enabled her to move forward against overwhelming adversity and thus to experience the amazing providence of God. Ruth did indeed suffer great hardship without becoming bitter, and was rewarded for her faithfulness by being **included in the lineage of Christ**.

<u>Naomi,</u> after losing husband and two sons, returned to her homeland and once again found herself under God's protection. She had a **bout with bitterness** (Ruth 1:20-21), but through her faith, Naomi chose a right relationship with God and others, experiencing again joy and fulfillment. She was not controlled by her

circumstances and yielded to God's sovereign grace and plan for her life (Ruth 4:13-17).

Another dynamic of bitterness: if in our unhealthy ways of processing it, we control, bury, or stifle - we do the

| Stifled anger. |
| Stifled love. |

cessing it, we control, bury, or stifle - we do the same to our positive emotions. We naturally control, bury and stifle love, joy, excitement, etc.

One fulfilling aspect of my counseling practice is to watch people become **more loving as they begin to resolve anger.** As they are freeing themselves up from the controls of anger, they are also releasing the ability to be able to express more love, care, and tenderness toward others.

S.I. McMillen, a physician skillful in writing as well as in practicing medicine, speaks of the devastating effect of bitterness turned into hatred. In "None of These Diseases", he wrote:

> "**The moment I start hating a man, I become his slave.** I can't enjoy my work and more because he even <u>controls my thoughts</u>. My resentments produce too many **stress hormones** in my body and I become <u>fatigued</u> after only a few hours of work. The work I formerly enjoyed is

| I become a slave |
| to whomever |
| I carry bitterness |

> now <u>drudgery.</u>. Even vacations cease to give me pleasure. It may be a luxurious car that I drive along a lake fringed with the autumn beauty of maple, oak and birth. As far as my experience of pleasure is concerned, I might as well be driving a wagon in mud and rain. The <u>**man I hate hounds me wherever I go**</u>. I can't escape his tyrannical grasp on my mind. When the waiter serves me porterhouse steak with french fries, asparagus, crisp salad and strawberry shortcake smothered with ice cream, it might as well be stale bread and water. My teeth chew the food and I swallow it, but the <u>**man I hate will not permit me to enjoy**</u> it. The man I hate may be miles from

41

my bedroom; but more cruel than any slave driver, he whips my thoughts into such a frenzy that my innerspring mattress becomes a rack of torture. The lowliest of serfs can sleep, but not I. I really must acknowledge the fact that **I am a slave to every man on whom I pour the vials of my wrath.**"

Bitterness may not kill the body (though it could), but it definitely kills the spirit. It kills enjoyment of life.

Death, bitterness and now the third result of unresolved anger:

☞ Anxiety

A young lady sat in my office, shaking. She was not afraid. Not sick. Not cold. She was angry. Having talked with her previously, I knew that her missionary parents had trained her well to bury all negative feelings: "Anger is not Christ like - stifle it."

When she had been sent to missionary boarding school at a young age, she perceived this forced separation as rejection. "**Mom and Dad had time for everyone but me. They even shipped me off to boarding school when I was seven.**"

Rejection and bitterness, buried, began to grow. She was married at the time she came to see me. Her husband was very passive and she had to make all the family decisions. She had to run the household. His philosophy, like many men, was "I bring home the bacon. You prepare it."

No sharing. Very little unity. He wasn't sensitive to her emotional needs. Rejection, again and again. More bitterness - buried. And there she sat, **shaking life a leaf.** I had a towel in my desk. I folded and rolled it, gave it to her, and said, "This towel represents your husband's neck." Before she could even

Towel Therapy: ONE WRUNG NECK!

think of what was happening, she was grasping the towel with both hands in a wringing motion with all her strength. A couple seconds later she realized the dynamics of her action and said, "Dr. Burwick, **I didn't realize how I hated Jim.**"

Her shaking stopped immediately and she began the process of resolving the angry spirit she had been carrying for years, towards parents, husband and other significant people.

Anger is the precipitator of much of our anxiety. It can also be a source for personality disorder.

☛ Personality Disorders

The term "personality disorder" has been defined as **abnormalities relating to personality traits. It usually demonstrates itself by a rigid, fixedness.** Like the very rigid person who says, "No" to everything.

| Kids have negative dad murdered. |

A father in New York was murdered. His two children, ages ten and twelve, **hired a professional killer for 50 dollars** to do away with him. Why?

The children indicated: "All Dad said was 'No' to everything we asked of him. We couldn't take it any more." His rigid, negative personalty culminated in his premature death.

Personality disorder is sometimes exposed through a **fixed trait of sarcasm, bitter words, cynical attitude, criticizing and putting others down.** These people, sometimes labeled "borderline personality," have **very little success at building relationships**.

Saccharine sweetness is a disorder and is often a cover-up for anger. The one who is outwardly very, very sweet is often one with much pent-up anger.

Unresolved anger is <u>one of many components</u> that cause personality disorders. It is also a chief contributor to depression.

☛ Depression

It has been said that ***<u>depression is anger that has lost its enthusiasm</u>***. The intense outward feelings of rage have been muzzled and subdued, but they have gone underground, brewing their depressive stew.

Depression is the **leading malady that brings people to my**

*I wasn't angry,
I was fed up*

counseling office. In the thousands of cases of depression I've treated, anger was the leading cause. (**Guilt** comes in a very distant second.)

There are many **other causes for depression** - hormone imbalance, thyroid dysfunction, side-effects of some medications, stress, loss, failure, lack of sunlight, and others. However, in my experience, **anger is the chief culprit**. Continued anger produces biochemical changes in the brain that, in a sense, slows down the "electrical system" resulting in depression. This, not being a research paper, I will not elaborate on the organic process.

The first step in treating depression is not to run to the doctor for medication. It is becoming culturally acceptable to **live better chemically** - while all along, not facing what is the most common cause: "Am I angry at someone?"

Medication is appropriate if the cloud of depression has so engulfed a person that functioning responsibly seems impossible. However, underlying issues must be faced. Rare is the depression that is strictly organically caused. For example, depression is reported to be one of the first signs of pancreatic cancer. In that case anger is obviously not an issue.

Carl didn't have cancer but he definitely displayed an **emotional "cancer."** He could hardly drag his body into my office. "I'm on antidepressants but they're not helping," reported the sloppily-dressed, middle-aged man. Upon questioning, Carl related a childhood story of tremendous emotional and physical abuse and abandonment by his mother. **Rage was his weapon.**

DEPRESSION: Imploded Anger.

At the age of 12, after a severe whipping he told his stepfather he'd kill him if he touched him again. None of his peers would tangle with Carl because of his fighting rage.

He basically took care of himself, age 12 on. As a college student, Carl became a Christian. The good news of love and grace was so refreshing to him that he jumped into the main stream of it wholeheartedly. Maybe too much. When his temper would flare, he would quickly deny that it was there as a means of subduing it. Carl reported, "**I wanted to be a godly young man and I knew that a raging temper was antithetical to what I wanted to be. I buried it. Stuffed it.**"

Carl did this so well that before long the anger that previously exploded, now imploded. Depression was the result.

Anger can also camouflage depression.

Dr. Archibald Hart, writing in "Christian Counseling Connection," says that explosive **anger has an underlying biochemistry that acts as a powerful, yet temporary, antidepressant.** "If you find yourself getting angry a lot, especially if this anger leads to violent emotional or physical acting out, you need to carefully consider the possibility of some underlying depression." He suggests antidepressant medication and cognitive therapy for treatment.

Listing all these results of unresolved anger is becoming depressing! I'd rather move on to resolution. And you, the reader, might be thinking of moving on to the next chapter. However, it is important to see the far-reaching effects our topic produces. Mental problems, next.

☛ Mental Problems

Most mental symptoms have a component of pent-up anger - obsessive compulsions, phobias, fantasies, schizophrenia and more.

When a person comes into my office with these kinds of symptoms, talking weirdly or hearing bells or voices, I say, "I'm sure what you are hearing and seeing seems real, but it is not. Your mind is playing tricks on you. We're wasting time talking about such things. Let's get at the root issues."

A <u>frequent</u> **significant underlying cause is unresolved anger.** As it is processed, the mental symptoms begin to fade.

Sometimes emotional or mental healing can be very quick. Pam, though a devoted Christian and very involved in her church, reported for counseling with **obsessive vulgar thoughts** toward God. They became worse when she went to church or read her Bible. Compounding the problem, she worked as a part time church secretary. The first psychologist told her to stay away from church and quit reading her Bible. That was his remedy!

> The remedy: Quit church and quit reading the Bible! Oh?

Hearing that I was a Christian counselor, she shared her story with me. "When I was nine years old, dad left. I lived with Mom who would have boyfriends spend the night. They would take advantage of me. **I liked the attention but knew there was something wrong with what was going on.** Some mornings I would have to help my drunken, beat-up mom up from the floor, where she had been left by her lover of the night."

> **Role reversal took place at a young age.**
> **Mary felt she had to take care of her mother.**
> **Her own abuse felt normal.**

Anger was an appropriate emotion for her to feel against those men and at her mother for not protecting her. That was a tough challenge for Mary. "The Bible tells me I am to honor my parents. **How is getting angry at mother honoring her?**" she asked.

I explained that getting angry wasn't the issue. The issue was the challenge to face the anger that was legitimately there. **Honoring her mother would be honestly facing reality and processing it in a healthy way** (which we'll talk about later in the book.)

"But that can't be the source of my obsessive vulgar thoughts toward God," the 48-year-old lady exclaimed. "These thoughts just started a few months ago. My abuse began nearly 40 years ago."

We kept digging. "What happened a few months ago that could have been traumatic to you," I asked. After a lengthy pause and with some chagrin, Pam related how she had found a peep hole in her pastor's closet that looked into her office.

Pastoral Peeping "Paul" "He would ask me to bring a change of clothes to the office so we could do yard work around the church in the afternoons. I'd lock the door and change clothes in my office. Dr. Burwick, I've never been so hurt and disappointed in a man. My pastor peeking at me when I dressed!"

Pam was a person, who like Carl, **wanted so badly to be a good Christian that she denied any feelings of anger. She felt she couldn't be a good Christian and be angry.** "Besides," she said, "How can I be angry at a pastor who I dearly love and respect?" But, she was being abused, looked upon as an object for a man's sexual pleasure. There should be a healthy anger toward that pastor. **Respect for his position is appropriate, but not for him as a peeping tom.**

To top it off, she had a husband who was a wonderful, sweet man. But so passive he wouldn't make decisions, take charge or even do anything about the peeping pastor. "How can I be angry at such a nice man," was her justification.

Vulgar thoughts dissipated quickly. As Pam began to face her normal, human feelings and work through them, her obsessive vulgar thoughts toward God dissipated, and rather quickly.

Another mental disorder is called **conversion hysteria.** One man's anger toward his wife was grotesque and deep, never having been resolved. Out of the blue, one day he had an urge to **pick up a knife and stab her.** Instead of facing what was going on inside, an unconscious reaction paralyzed the arm he would have used to stab her. This paralysis was a classic example of conversion hysteria.

Are guilt and anger related? Let's take a peek.

☞ Guilt

Guilt has to be punished. It seems to be an unwritten law. The bank robber often leaves a trail, as if to say, "catch me. I'm guilty." The self punishment that often takes place when guilt isn't resolved can become a masochistic execution in self flagellation.

Unresolved anger is one of the causes of guilt. This can underlie food-related symptoms as in eating too much or too little. The latter is the person who refuses to eat or who eats and then induces vomiting until he or she becomes thinner and thinner.

One person who started at 130 pounds finally died of starvation at the weight of sixty pounds. Anger within was not faced, was not resolved, which caused guilt feelings. The subconscious reasoning continued that the guilt had to be punished, and punishment could be starving oneself. Anorexia nervosa is the medical term.

Sharon was a highly intelligent, articulate seventeen-year-old, who nearly died at half her normal body weight. She gave me permission to tell her story. Some time after her stay in the intensive care unit to treat the anorexia nervosa, we met and began to penetrate the walls of insecurity and masked bitterness that had been built around this lovely girl.

Weeks lapsed into months, **forced feedings, hospitalizations,** some temporary breakthroughs in counseling, but always an underlying stubbornness, rebellious spirit and manipulation. This bright teen who even articulated all the right spiritual things to say, was even picked up for shop lifting.

| A diet of railroad spikes. |

To illustrate her deviousness, Sharon's physician had her on a two pounds-per-week weight gain plan. After a few weeks, the doctor noticed she was getting thinner and thinner, yet the scales indicated a gain of two pounds per week.

Her family lived near railroad tracks. Can you guess what her ploy was? On that fateful day of discovery, the nurse asked her to strip before the weigh-in. **Sewn to her slip were eighteen pounds of railroad spikes.**

Many similar escapades led to that one Saturday morning when she finally saw that she was missing out on life. She **began to resolve the inner dynamics of which anger was a part.** She gained weight and grew into a delightful, well-adjusted person.

However, we are creatures of habit and **unless healthy ways of thinking and living are maintained, we can slip back into old destructive patterns**. Sharon did. She and her family moved shortly after counseling. I didn't see her until years later when I found her to be back into her destructive eating patterns relishing her ability to "control" her weight. Anger, deceit, manipulation, rebellion, insecurity had not been faced and resolved. Sharon lived a miserable life.

"All right, already, Burwick. That's enough negative stuff. Let's move on."

I don't blame you. This is getting heavy. But it is important to be well informed. Bear with me and examine:

☞ **Psychosomatic Illness** (bodily disorder with mental origin)

Dr. Theodore Rubin's <u>Angry Book</u> does an excellent job of explaining the psychosomatic dynamics of anger" Briefly, he says:

> "The ears receive sound waves; the eyes receive light waves that convey messages to the brain in which is integrated information that makes us angry. This feeling is felt by the entire body. Messages are sent out by chemical changes in nerves so that various hormones are excreted: <u>heart-rate</u> <u>changes</u>, the **diameter of blood vessels change**, and so on. **These effects in turn affect the skin, musculature, the digestive tract, the lungs - all systems and organs of the body**. Messages that are smooth and free flowing will see healthy expression; messages that are polluted will have poisonous physical repercussions."

Polluted messages produce poisonous fruits.

A psychosomatic illness is still an illness! A stomach <u>ulcer</u> hurts. If there is a perforation, the person is in medical danger.

Causes are numerous, but one is anger. Medication can relieve symptoms. Surgery may be necessary, but the underlying cause, if emotional based, must be resolved.

It is amazing how often **migraines** subside after a good, quick, temper tantrum. Many **asthmatics** experience relief as they learn to cry. **Beethoven** is thought to have brought on his own **deafness** by a fit of temper.

The following information from a mental health journal is sobering. It states that

doctors are warning people who grimly suppress their emotions, and people who vent every emotion, are more likely to experience **cancer** than people who are moderate but consistent in expressing how they honestly feel. In other words,

both extremes of burying everything or
venting everything can be equally dangerous.

Anger appears to be one of the precipitating causes of **arthritis**. A beautiful young woman sat in my office with the twisted, swollen joints of rheumatoid arthritis. It had begun two years previously, when she became a Christian. The tremendously volatile temper she had carried as a teenager was not in keeping with her view of what a Christian ought to be, so she buried the temper. Within weeks, arthritis began.

Another woman was normal until she caught her husband in bed with another woman. Her arthritis flared so fast that she was in a wheelchair within thirty days.

Anger outbursts kill muscle fibers in a person's heart. It can cause **high blood pressure**, **atherosclerosis** (the blocking of blood flow in arteries,) **kidney damage**, elevation of **cholesterol**, **heart fibrillation**, and a host of other physical dis-eases.

Not only problems within, but problems without as we see next in:

☞ Relational problems

The story is told of a little boy who had a bad temper. His father gave him a bag of nails and told him every time he lost his temper, he must hammer a nail into the back of the fence. The first day the boy had driven 37 nails into the fence. Over the next few weeks, as he learned to control his anger, the number of nails hammered daily gradually dwindled down. He discovered it was easier to hold his temper than to drive nails into the fence.

ANGER-INDUCED RELATIONAL WOUNDS.

Finally the day came when the boy didn't lose his temper at all. He told his father about it and the father suggested that the boy now pull out one nail for each day that he was able to hold his temper. The days passed and the young boy was finally able to tell his father that all the nails were gone.

The father took his son by the hand and led him to the fence. He said, "You have done well, my son, but look at the holes in the fence. The fence will never be the same. When you say things in anger, they leave a scar just like this one. You can put a knife in a man and draw it out. It won't matter how many times you say I'm sorry, the wound is still there. A verbal wound is as bad as a physical one. Friends are a very rare jewel indeed. They make you smile and encourage you to succeed. They lend an ear, they share words of praise and they always want to open their hearts to us.

Nothing more needs to be said about the effects of anger on relationships. We've all experienced the devastation of a hurtful word. And, the one you care about the most can hurt you the deepest! Even a mother to her inutero baby.

From Mom to the womb

☞ Babies Affected

It is believed that an expectant mother who nurses a chronic angry spirit, produces hormones causing an unbalanced mixture of catecholamines to be introduced into the baby's bloodstream. Results? Possible physical or emotional problems in the baby after birth.

I know. You're tired of reading all this negative stuff. I'm tired of writing it. My purpose is to possibly catch someone's attention who may be struggling with an anger-induced issue and not recognize the possible source. **This could set someone free.** So I continue:

☛ Other Symptoms

Other symptoms of anger can be **Aggression**. The angry person can be an aggressive identifier such as the owner of a huge, vicious dog; or a little old lady viewing a wrestling match from the front row yelling, "Kill him."

Accident proneness. Anger held in often results in <u>subconscious self-punishment</u> as in the careless use of knives, guns, machinery or automobiles. A clumsy, accident-prone person may really be an angry person.

Workaholism. The <u>overindulgent</u> person is often one who escapes resolving anger (or other inner turmoil) through work, sports, and other activities. When a person is always busy, he doesn't have to stop and face what might be churning inside.

Elephant mind. "Do you remember twenty-five years ago on our honeymoon when you watched TV instead of celebrating our marriage?" The person who never forgets an offense.

Giggling at the wrong time; **chronic forgetting**; **talking out loud** during movies and plays; **bumping** into people; **habitual lateness**; **embarrassing a companion**; **giving misinformation**; or a sudden attack of **stupidity**, all of these can signal unresolved anger.

Very <u>subtle symptoms</u> can appear, such as the "Don't worry about me" manipulation. This is typified by the angry, insecure parent who has a hard time cutting the apron strings, and says, "Sure you can go out on a date. Don't worry about me, even though I might be dead by the time you get back."

The **malicious gossip** is an angry person. **Dreams of violence and death**, or <u>fantasies</u> of violence or death are anger symptoms, as is chronic, **malicious joking**.

53

I blew up

Others who may be angry are the "peace-keepers," who never say a harsh word. The sexually provocative may be trying to get back at a mate or lead a man on to get even with men.

The person who retreats or withdraws, the intolerant person, the pessimist, any of these may be an angry person.

The person with much distrust; the one who is seldom pleased; the person with no joy; the bore, the person who uses drugs, the maniac driver, or the teeth grinder.

| Self-destructive teeth grinder |

One of my angry clients shared his teeth-grinding experience. He had, over the past ten years, developed two stress-related physiological problems resulting in surgery. Over the years, because of unresolved emotional problems, (including anger), it became a habit for him to clench his teeth.

The repeated hard bite possibly triggered growth of additional bone about the upper and lower jaw in an effort to help the jaw to sustain the added forces. Also, the teeth, especially in the front of the mouth, were worn down so much that a special retainer had to be made to prevent him from clenching his teeth.

The strain, due to the oversized jaw, caused the gums to pull away from the teeth, and periodontal disease, an infection of the gum tissue, developed. Toxins from the infection reduced his body health in general. The gum disease was hastened by inconsistent dental preventative maintenance during periods of prolonged depression. In short, the teeth grinder was literally destroying himself.

Anger produces more immediate effects on the body's chemical balance than any other emotion. While the feeling may pass quickly, the damage, like a hurricane, is devastating.

There can be other causes for all the above listings, but
**pent-up anger is probably the leading cause
of disease and death.**

Some **chiropractors** say, "If you're sick you're out of adjustment."
Some **nutritionists** say, "If you are sick, you are not eating right."
Let us not be as dogmatic, but we should ask,
"Is my malady caused by pent-up anger?"

Follow me to the next chapter and see if you can identify with anger at a deeper level then you've experienced previously.

Scripture:
"See to it that no one misses the grace of God and that <u>no bitter root grows</u> up to cause trouble and defile many." (Hebrews 12:15).

Prayer:
Father, Show me. Does any of this chapter apply to me? Are any of the personal or interpersonal challenges I'm facing linked to unresolved anger?

Exercise:
Consider going back through the chapter and listing here possible anger-rooted results in your life.

Five
Are You Ticked, Hot, Or Just Irritated
Recognizing Anger

For every minute you remain angry, you give up sixty seconds of peace of mind. Emerson

Possibly you've related to some of the signs of anger in the past chapters. Or your anger is the rage type that everyone near you recognizes. You **are aware** of the challenges you face. However, a **large percentage of people hide or deny their anger** causing vocational, personal and interpersonal dysfunction that can be catastrophic in results.

The church, and society in general, often teaches us to avoid anger and especially to avoid expressing it. Hiding it can be strictly unconscious. Some folk are just not aware of packing a suitcase of anger. Consequently, being unaware of personal anger does not mean that you are not angry. **Anger that you are not aware of can be the most damaging to yourself and others** close to you. It will come out somehow!

Anger can be likened to the smoke of a wood-burning fireplace. The normal expression of smoke is up through the chimney. If the passage way is blocked, or an imperfect draft exists, smoke will expel itself out the opening in a most unpleasant way, choking those in the room.

> Fireplace anger chokes

If you were taught to **stifle anger, the smoke chokes you**. If you were taught to **rage, the smoke chokes relationships and you**.

Socrates said,
> **"An unexamined life is not worth living."**

King David said,
> **"Search me, oh God."**

57

Let's engage in some __healthy self exploration__. Remember the word "balance."

> Constant "navel-gazing" can create some terrible self-centeredness.
>
> But no introspection leads to a myriad of "sins."

We're suggesting an exercise that enhances our ability to observe attitudes and behavior that contaminate godliness. To accomplish this, we must be willing to see our ungodliness - our pride, concealed wounds, sophisticated pettiness and ugly demandingness. Sometimes this kind of observation doesn't present a pretty sight. As an athletic coach might say:

"It's check-up time."

The following evaluation has been adapted from my counseling experience and numerous articles and web sites. It is helpful to evaluate oneself, but sometimes more helpful to have **someone close to you authentically go through the list with you. Do you have someone who could give you such a love gift?**

Physical signs of Anger

Some of these have already been mentioned in a previous chapter. Remember, anger is not the only cause for the following!

1. **Psychosomatic illness** (as mentioned in the previous chapter)
2. Tone of **voice gets louder** or **speech more rapid** when discussing a controversial topic
3. **Aggressively competitive** even when playing for fun
4. Volcanic **explosions**
5. Quick to **defend oneself**
6. Having to be right. **My way is the only way**
7. Controlling others with **commanding demands**
8. Controlling others with **guilt**
9. Controlling others by **physical force**
10. **Gossiping** that harms others

11. Anger has **pushed friends and loved ones away**
12. Habitual **lateness**
13. Habitual **procrastination**
14. **Saccharine sweet** politeness
15. **Smiling while emotionally hurting**
16. **Over-controlled speaking voice**
17. **Sleep** disturbance
18. Getting **tired more easily** than usual
19. **Clenched jaws**, teeth grinding, especially while sleeping
20. **Chronically stiff or sore** neck or shoulder muscles
21. **Red blotches** on the neck when discussing a conflict
22. **Drumming** with fingers
23. Shortened breath, **heavy breathing**
24. **Stomach** tightness
25. **Sweaty palms**
26. **Rapid heart beat**
27. Pounding in the head
28. **Shaking uncontrollably**
29. Blushing
30. Apologizing when none is asked for

Remember, it is check-up time

Emotional signs of anger

1. **Envying others**, especially those having a softer life
2. **Misdirected anger** (anger at someone with whom you should not be angry)
3. **Moodiness**, brooding, sullenness
4. **Intolerance**, impatience
5. **Distrust**
6. Enjoying sadistic or **ironic humor**
7. **Critical** of others who don't agree with me
8. **Withdrawal**, shutting down of communication with a person
9. **Easily annoyed** when someone is not sensitive to my needs
10. **Irritated easily** at those who refuse to admit their mistakes
11. **Hold grudges** (don't easily forgive when someone wrongs me)

12. I sometimes feel **life is not fair.**
13. I sometimes **blame others** for my troubles
14. **Easily frustrated** when things don't go my way
15. **Plotting harm** against another
16. Joyless, **lack of pleasure in activities**
17. Tendency to be real **negative**
18. **Frightening dreams**

> Are you
> seeing
> anything
> that applies
> to you?

Again, may I repeat, **these symptoms don't always signal anger.** For example, procrastination can be caused by laziness. It can be caused by fear of failure. But sometimes people use procrastination to get even, to get under the skin of someone else. It is a subtle way to express anger - often unconsciously.

The first step in considering anger is to recognize it. These two lists can be used in different manners.

- ❖ As a **discussion guide** between two friends or family members who dare to be lovingly and encouragingly authentic with each other.
- ❖ As a **small group discussion** guide where members have covenanted to be compassionately honest and vulnerable with each other.
- ❖ As a **numerical tool** where a number from 1 to 10 is associated with each item.

There is no good or bad score. But a consistent high score can identify that anger is a challenge.

Other Resources

Les Carter and Frank Minirth produced "The Anger Workbook" which is an excellent source to help identify personal anger. (Thomas Nelson Publishers.)

The Internet provides anger testing.
Some sources:

> www.queendom.com/cgi-bin/tests/anger.cgi.
> www.abetterworkplace.com/anger_eval.html
> www.midtowncounseling.com/generic.jhtml?pid=2

Though tests of this nature may not be completely accurate, they can enhance insight into our anger issues.

Hopefully this chapter has given you more insights into yourself and will bring you greater physical, emotional, spiritual and relational freedom as the principles of the following chapters in anger resolution are integrated.

Scripture:

Psalm 139:23-24 *Search me, O God, and know my heart; test me and know my anxious thoughts. See if there any offensive way in me, and lead me in the way everlasting.*

Prayer:

Father, I've been reading a lot about symptoms of anger. Am I missing anything? Something I'm not seeing? Anything else that hasn't been described that can apply to me?

_____

_____

_____

Exercise:

What do the following passages of Scripture say to you?

Ephesians 4:31 _____

_____

_____

Colossians 3:8 _____

_____

_____

2 Corinthians 12:20 and Galatians 5:20-21 _____

_____

_____

Ephesians 4:26 _____

_____

_____

Matthew 5:21-22 _____

_____

_____

Six

The Gift of Anger

Benefits of Anger

Anger is often a sign of ingratitude

"**How can anger be a gift**," you may ask, "when a previous chapter detailed its destructiveness?"

Just as athletes do stretching exercises before a contest to better prepare themselves and to prevent injury, let's do some mental stretching as we endeavor to grasp how anger can be a **gift for our personal growth.**

Anger is a Signal

Just as indicator lights on a car's dashboard signal to the driver the motor's dysfunction, so also, anger signals to us that something "under the hood" needs to be checked. What can I learn about myself as a result of detecting anger? What is my anger telling me about me?

Determine first the anger label

Is it "holy anger?" Healthy anger? Or is it **unhealthy anger?**

Holy anger

Recall with me that **holy anger** is demonstrated by God against disobedience and rebellion, (Numbers 25:1-9; Ephesians 5:6); idolatry (Judges 2:10-15); ingratitude and complaining (Numbers 11:1-33); and also many other issues.

"Holy" Anger Test

Relating to God's anger is difficult because of our human world view. Probably the closest we can come is viewing Moses breaking the tablets containing the ten commandments. His was an anger at the Israelites for worshipping a golden calf (Exodus 32:19). What angered God, angered Moses.

63

That is the **holy anger test**:
   does **what angers you, also anger God?**

Is the anger rooted in a perceived injustice to myself or is it in my sensitivity to injustice toward other people?

A check point though. How do you handle holy anger? Not like Absalom, I hope. Second Samuel 13 tells the story of Amnon raping his half sister, Tamar. Her brother, Absalom "hated him with a deep hatred" and nursed that hatred for two years until he arranged for Amnon's murder.

| Holy Anger: |
| Constructive |
| or |
| Destructive |

God certainly is angry with a man who rapes a woman. Was Absalom's anger "holy" anger? Yes. Anger must be expressed, but not in an Absalom unholy way.

Are you angry at physicians who murder babies (abortion)? That is holy anger. How do you express it? Blow away the doctor or the building? No! Send a package laced with anthrax to the place of abortion? Nope! That's **holy anger handled in unholy ways.**

Anger towards abortion has been expressed in many creative, positive ways. **Praying** for the doctors, the nurses and the victims. **Peaceful marches and sit-ins. Legal and political paths.** Helping **fund homes for unwed mothers. Volunteering at clinics** that promote live babies instead of death.

   Christ expressed holy anger through:
      sorrow (Matthew 23:37-39);
      verbal confrontation (Matthew chapter 23);
      physical confrontation (Matthew 21:12-13).
Christ's anger was not from a selfish, passionate: "I didn't get my way" kind of anger, but anger at church leaders who were hypocritical or abusing the people. His had a holy purpose.

Our holy anger must be expressed constructively.
It becomes unholy anger if it is handled with vengeance
or harbored without doing something productive with it.

Tom White, director of Frontline Ministries, relates his anger story. May it challenge each of us.

> "Some years back, I was co-facilitating a Prayer Summit with a brother. In an evening session, in my estimation, he really missed the mark and moved more in his own soul power and desire than in the Spirit. As I sat alongside him the **judgment and irritation built like hot lava in a volcano.** When we got into our room, I let my irritation spill over. **I felt justified, but my attitude wounded his spirit.**

> "Three weeks later, on assignment in Australia, in another Summit, the Spirit

Holy Anger Gone Awry

> made it clear that I had an anger problem. It was my time to get real. Fasting for a day, I asked the Lord to bring my impatience and irritation to the Cross, and to give me a greater grace of forbearance. I was repulsed enough by my reactions to be ready for an 'overhaul.'

> "The Holy Spirit brought a decrease of my Adamic self-life ... and an increased capacity of Jesus' life. I e-mailed my brother to confess my sin and seek his forgiveness. Two weeks later **I drove ninety miles to follow this up with a face-to-face.** Our relationship quickly grew to a deeper, more authentic level."

Tom demonstrated a holy anger gone awry and then resolution for it. Anger label number one: holy anger. Now look at label two: **healthy anger.**

Healthy Anger

Like holy anger, **healthy anger is an appropriate response** that probably contains some holy in it. Let me explain. As mentioned in chapter one, people who have been sexually abused in childhood often carry diffused feelings about the abuse and don't connect with an appropriate anger toward the perpetrator. **The anger lies hidden within and surfaces indirectly.**

RATIONALIZE
ANGER AND DIE

Depression rained on Tim's parade. "Yes, Dad was very verbally abusive, but he couldn't help it," Tim reported in our first counseling session. "A war wound destroyed him mentally and at times he was just crazy. He couldn't help berating me, telling me I'd never amount to anything and that I'd mess up a free lunch."

Tim, **instead of feeling a normal resentment toward his dad for the abuse, rationalized for him.** Consequently the anger buried itself deeply within, totally unrecognizable, and surfaced through depression and a "loser" mentality. Though Tim was an extremely intelligent, capable man, he hadn't found success because of the emotional link to his dad's judgment: "you'll never amount to anything."

He had to allow himself the right to **face his normal human emotion of anger at a cruel dad, no matter the father's situation.** Anger had to be faced squarely at his mother for not protecting him from his dad. Healthy anger then had to be processed in constructive ways, which we'll discuss in the next chapter.

Healthy anger used very productively.

Another example of healthy anger is that experienced when danger is imminent. An intruder entering your house in the dark of night brandishing a pistol is not there to participate in a Home Bible Study. You are in danger. Your family is in danger. **Healthy anger wells up inside producing sufficient adrenaline to perform super human acts to protect your family.**

Many have been the stories of young male intruders who have engaged in combat with 70 plus year old women in their homes, met their match and to save their skin, fled the scene.

Holy anger. Healthy anger. Now, label three: unhealthy anger.

Unhealthy Anger

Remember we are using anger as an indicator light on the dashboard, encouraging us to look under the hood. From a quarter of a century of counseling and my 67 years of living, I can comfortably say,

95% of our anger
is not holy anger
or healthy anger
but unhealthy anger.

So, how can unhealthy anger, as destructive as it is, be a signal for a person's benefit?

Answer: **it can teach us about ourselves**.

Anger often reveals how we **feel and think about ourselves** and how important we have made **our own ideas and insight**. Anger usually has a

| Anger is a TEACHER |

destructive underlying issue, that once we identify, can be processed for healthy, maturing change.

<u>For those of us who desire personal growth, anger has something valuable to teach us</u>. It can help us heal.

If there is an inordinate amount of anger surfacing to a present situation or person, chances are that we're either **experiencing a generalized stressful time** and are more easily agitated; or, the extra amount of anger surfacing signals to us that the current person is hooking into **something unresolved from the past**.

Mary's anger signal (obsessive vulgar thoughts toward God) <u>pointed her inward and backward to face the deep pain</u> she had unknowingly carried for years. As she allowed herself to face the intensity and process the pain in a Biblical fashion, great inner healing ensued.

Anger can reveal a threat.

The question is this kind of anger indicating a real threat or imaginary? Misunderstanding another's intentions or misinterpreting their actions, may lead to <u>anger of an imaginary threat</u>. The Bible says: "speak the truth in love." It is at times appropriate to communicate something like:

> "What you said came across to me as a real put-down. I don't know if you meant it that way or not. I don't want to be angry with you. May we talk about it?"

| Communication |
| boundaries |
| established |

An adult child who says: "Dad, I'll communicate with you but I have to set boundaries for my **psychological health**. You may only answer my questions and I want no commentary." This rigid guideline seems very restrictive, but for the child's sake, the father adheres. He understands that the child is going through an angry process, with Dad as the focal point. He sees himself as a threat and understands that a commentary would produce more anger and more pain.

Anger can reveal exaggeration

When anger has built up inside of a person, he/she tends to think in exaggerated terms that can cause undo relational conflict. Examples: "He is always late. He is never a thoughtful person."

Though tardiness and thoughtlessness can be real problems, to use the <u>words "always" and "never" usually inflame</u> the communication and the exaggeration leads to greater conflict, harder to work through.

Anger can reveal an out-of-control lifestyle

Stress can be used productively. It can help us **prepare for a test.** It can **heighten the senses to perform in tiptop shape.** But too much stress, especially that which our culture encourages, can be very debilitating.

Many families are either single-parented or child-oriented.

| Rearrange your priority structure |

Most single parents are under great stress as they try to be mom and dad to the child. Parents who operate a child-oriented household usually are so involved in pleasing their children, that they have little time for themselves or for each other. The stress is great. Being easily irritated or raging over minutia is anger's signal: bring control into your life. Rearrange your priority structure.

Anger reveals a hidden vow

Often the counselor hears, "**I'm never going to be an angry person like my father.**" This is an inner vow that is often made as a child. I don't understand the dynamics of it, but that kind of <u>vow</u> <u>seems to link that person to the perpetrator</u> and the child becomes like the parent - angry.

An inner vow must be faced and broken by a prayer that renounces that mindset, or the anger problem will continue.

Anger reveals manipulation

Are you **manipulating through anger to get your way?** Results vary. Sometimes manipulation can achieve temporary results.<u> An angry, manipulative voice can make its recipient submit to the order</u>. The outcome is usually counterproductive, in that long lasting behavioral change rarely takes place.

Anger reveals guilt

Guilt can be so subtle. The ultimate guilt situations I've seen are those people who have walked closely with God but in later years drift and sometimes declare "there is no God." I found this especially true while doing **research on why pastors' children abuse drugs and alcohol.** (www.notalone.org)

A high percentage of these children, even exposed to the Good News, claimed they had no guilt during their chemical-abusive experience. Invariably, this person had wandered into a little disobedience to God's guidelines. The wandering evolves into a considerable prodigal behavior. To justify the behavior, the person begins to question if there is God. **To avoid the pang of conscious guilt, declaration is made, "There is no God."** And <u>anger, at life in general, is often a camouflage, hiding the real issue</u> - guilt.

Anger reveals fear

Fear of **losing control** of a situation.

Fear of **not being in control**.

Fear of **losing a person's love**.

Fear of the **future**.

Fear of **powerlessness**.

Many different fears can produce anger. <u>Some professionals go so far as to say that fear is the underlying issue causing all anger</u>.

Anger reveals distorted self esteem

Feelings of inadequacy, inferiority and insecurity are, in my opinion, the<u> second leading cause of destructive anger.</u> Just as an auctioneer cries out the value of an item to potential buyers, so do **we esteem the value of our personhood, evaluating how interpersonal interchanges effect our sense of well being.** Much like fear, in our insecurity we become threatened by a person or situation, triggering an anger episode. For example, the insecure husband/father who is easily angered when family doesn't jump his hoops.

Anger reveals self-centeredness

The number one cause of unhealthy anger:

<u>I'm not getting my way</u> at the time I desire it.

Selfishness. We all have it. We all do it.

For some, it grows worse during the aging process. We've all seen the crotchety old people who are quick to bite others' heads off.

Others mellow out, becoming more comfortable with

70

themselves and life. **They've learned that richness of life comes from giving and not getting. They've allowed the hard knocks of life to make them better instead of bitter.** Selfishness diminishes with maturation. Less about which to be angry.

The gift of anger

It's not that we try hard not to be angry. Instead, we use our anger productively.

We can learn much about ourselves at the moment of anger or in retrospect as the flames have cooled and we think through it more logically.

> **What kind of anger was that?**
> **What have I learned about myself because of it?**
> **Am I processing it appropriately?**
> **How will I be a better person?**
> **How can I prepare for a similar situation in the future?**

Stick with me as we move on to the next section of study, "the remedy" for anger.

Scripture:

Psalm 19:12-13 (TLB): _But how can I ever know what sins are lurking in my heart? Cleanse me from these hidden faults. And keep me from deliberate wrongs; help me to stop doing them. Only then can I be free of guilt and innocent of some great crime._

Exercise:

As you read this chapter, what did you learn about yourself because of the signal of anger? List an example of a past holy anger.

_____

Did you express it? ____ How did you constructively express it?

_____

_____

Are you aware of any healthy anger lessons ? _____

_____

Sources for unhealthy anger can look so ugly. What did you observe that were some of the underlying issues in your anger? Expose some ugly!! _____

_____

_____

Prayer:

Father, instead of denying anger, instead of feeling guilty about anger, instead of allowing anger to control me, please empower me to see anger as a gift from which I can learn and be a more productive person for others and for myself. Teach me now as I examine the remedy for anger.

Part II
PROCESSING ANGER

Holding on to anger is like grasping a hot coal with the intent of throwing it at someone else; you are the one who gets burned.
Buddha

Anger has been identified. What's next?

We've already suggested **holy anger**, that though a very infrequent human experience, **must be expressed in some constructive way.** For if it is capped off, it can become vengeful and unholy.

Healthy anger is an appropriate anger usually directed toward an abuser. It is an anger that is often hidden (rationalized), **is not selfish based and must be processed in healthy ways.** We'll exam this procedure in the next chapter.

We'll then examine **unhealthy anger** and how it is processed, first looking at popular **management techniques, followed by Biblical resolution.**

C.S. Lewis, in his book <u>The Joyful Christian</u>, gives us a unique challenge in processing anger. He says,

> "One man may be so placed that **his anger sheds the blood of thousands,** and another so placed that **however angry he gets he will only be laughed at.** But the little mark on the soul may be much the same in both. Each has done something to himself which, unless he repents, will make it harder for him to keep out of the rage next time he is tempted, and will make the rage worse when he does fall into it. **Each of them, if he seriously turns to**

73

God, can have that twist in the central man straightened out again; each is, in the long run, doomed if he will not. The bigness or smallness of the thing, seen from the outside, is not what really matters."

Seven

Mad as Heaven

Handling Healthy Anger

No man can think clearly when his fists are clenched. G.J. Nathan

Healthy anger is an appropriate anger response toward a source of abuse, be it sexual, physical, emotional or spiritual. Let me explain.

Identifying healthy anger is often a struggle because it is usually camouflaged under some rationalization. "It wasn't that bad." "It was my fault." "But I love him," are common responses describing an abuse situation.

The typical counseling treatment plan begins with an encouragement to face the pain within. Usually healthy anger is all mixed up with guilt, rationalizations, and sometimes a pleasure component. (In sexual abuse, young bodies respond to sexual stimulation and young minds can perceive the attention as "love.")

I've found it helpful in counseling to work through each of the emotional issues, leaving anger to the last.

"Yes, your body responded to the stimulation," I challenge. "And for that you are feeling guilty. But it is a false guilt. God made our bodies to respond like yours did. However, for that person to stimulate you was for his pleasure, not for your fulfillment. He was wrong. He wronged you. I'm angry at him for how he abused you."

"But he loved me and I loved him," the client often says.

My response: "His abusing you was not love. And yes, you love(d) him. But remember:

The one you love the most can hurt you the worst and that can be to whom you carry the most resentment.

"But it was my fault. Maybe I lured him into it."

"No. A hundred times, NO. It was his problem. His lust prompted him to do what he did. A little boy or girl is not naturally wired to 'turn on' an older person. It is the abuser's problem, not yours."

"Now, let's deal with an emotion you should normally have toward the perpetrator:

Anger, resentment, bitterness, hate,
whatever label best fits your feelings."

The Three F's

A plan is developed that involves the three F's. *Face. Feel. Forgive.*

A healthy way I've found to face and feel is to write (journaling). Some people who have buried the anger so deeply have to begin with an intellectual approach: "based on the circumstances, this is what I should be feeling. I should be angry because …"

Follow this by a prayer something like, "God, help me to feel what I should naturally be feeling in this situation. Help me relive the experience to fully grasp the pain of it to prompt deep healing."

We don't ask God to conjure up what is not there. We just ask for a legitimate awareness of the pain that has been buried.

Such daily journaling, praying and possibly sharing it with someone trustworthy is the healthiest way I've found to encourage the facing and feeling dimension of processing healthy anger.

The third F, the forgiving process, has three components.

1. For my well-being, I must forgive.

2. Do I confront the perpetrator?

3. Do I have relationship with the abuser?

➤ Forgive

The depth of forgiving is directly proportionate to the depth of feeling of that which needs to be forgiven.

Feel the pain, the anger, the rage. Shallow feeling leads to a benign surface-forgiving that accomplishes but little on the road to freedom from physical, emotional, mental, relational and spiritual bondage.

The **process of forgiving** is one of the hardest challenges a person faces. Not only do you have the agony of reliving the pain, but then letting go of the enticing taste for vengeance.

We'll scrutinize more the forgiving process when we examine the resolution for past anger described in the next chapter.

➤ Confrontation?

"Do I confront the abuser?" is an oft repeated question I hear. Possibly. AA says, "If it hurts someone, don't." If the person is dead, the answer is obvious.

However, some people have found it helpful to go the graveyard and address the site where the person is buried and either read a prepared statement of confrontation or spontaneously say something like: "What you did was wrong (explaining what it was.) I have resented you deeply for taking advantage of me. I no longer want to hang on to those feelings toward you. I choose to let them go. I am in the process of forgiving you and expect that somehow God will even use your abuse of me for His glory and my good."

Martha had a tough challenge with a dead father. **He died while having sex with her.** "He brainwashed me into believing that being a good daughter was taking care of needs that his wife refused to meet. He'd get very violent to all of us if I didn't cooperate with him. I'm ashamed now but even as a single adult, I felt I had to take care of dad's sexual needs."

It took some time of intense counseling and prayer for her to be free from the ongoing emotional hurricane of shame, guilt and anger she was experiencing.

A gray area surfaces regarding whether to confront or not. If the abuser is living but wants no relationship with you, the answer is not as clear. Usually very little if anything is accomplished if you confront a person that wants nothing to do with you. It would create more hateful, dissident feelings that would heighten your own pain.

There is never a definite "yes" to the confrontation question, because you don't know the impact it will have on the abuser. It could send them over the edge, resulting in suicide. Would you be prepared for that?

The most affirmative "yes" is to the abuser who wants to maintain contact with you – possibly a family member or friend. For the greatest impact to be made for the speaker and the listener, one must go in the spirit of gentleness and humility (that comes through the forgiving process), combined with a demeanor of tough firmness sounding something like, "You abused me. You took advantage of me for your own gratification. What you did was wrong. There is no excuse. I am choosing to hold resentment against you no longer. I am in the process of forgiving you."

There are legal ramifications here also. Especially important is for the abuser to be removed from the home if the child he is abusing is still living at home. Authorities must be notified.

The next relational step is determined by the response of the abuser.

Do I have relationship with the abuser?

You may consider cautiously building a relationship if:

- ✔ the abuser accepts full responsibility for his actions;
- ✔ the abuser demonstrates a deep sorrow and repentance for his act;
- ✔ it appears he has not abused other people, or if he has, he has received in-depth therapy and demonstrates a repentant spirit.

Forgiving does not mean an automatic restoration of fellowship. The abuser typically denies or at best excuses his violation.

He is not to be trusted, and if there is relationship, it is with extreme caution and arms-length protection.

Many women find, as did Sue, that restoration is impossible. Sue confronted her father for his sexual abuse of her. He denied it, said she was making it up (and there are cases where this happens – either false memories, anger gone irrational or vengeance). Sue's father was heavily involved in church. She went to his pastor, laid out the clear evidence and encouraged the pastor to talk with her father. He did and the father explosively denied any sexual abuse and left the church. Both behaviors cemented in the pastor's mind that the man was, in fact, guilty and non-repentant. Sue had to break fellowship with her father for her and her children's protection.

Rachel, on the other hand, in confronting her father, found a man who acted sorry but still had an alluring look in his eyes. She maintained relationship with him but would not be alone with him in the house. He could not baby-sit her children.

In summary, do you get a little feel of healthy anger resolution? While writing this section, I talked to a man on the phone that was having trouble with healthy anger. His mother was a very troubled individual and caused him great pain as a child. His words linger in my ears, "I think anger killed my mom. I'm doing everything I can to avoid being like her."

His depression and anxiety, in my opinion, is from denial of healthy anger to an abusive mother and to other terrible abuse that he had experienced recently. His desire to avoid being like his mother, and in his great quest to be a godly man, he is denying instead of processing healthy anger.

And now to that most difficult, yet freeing, task – forgiving.

Scripture:
Matthew 6:15 But if you do not forgive men their sins, your Father will not forgive your sins.

Prayer:
Father, everyone has been hurt by someone. And I have hurt others, sometimes even unknowingly. Are there any relationships for which I need to make amends? Have I finished processing all of my healthy anger?

Exercise:
I notice that I have a tendency to cover healthy anger by (circle if applicable):

"He didn't mean it."

"But I love(d) him/her."

"She's not as bad as she used to be."

"He couldn't help it."

"That is the way she was treated as a kid also."

"She had good intentions."

"Other people have had it worse."

"Nothing hurts me. I can live above it."

"I've been treated worse."

Eight
I'll Forgive But I Won't Forget
Past Anger Resolution

He who has conquered anger, has conquered demons...
He who prays for his enemies can not be revengeful.
Evagrius Ponticus

Past anger. Wounds of the past. Hurtful rejections of yore. All are resolved in only one way: forgiving. We touched on this in the last chapter. Not much in life is tougher then thoroughly forgiving someone who has hurt us deeply.

The best of forgiving I see, even in the church,
is a desire to forget, not to intensely forgive.

Out of sight, out of mind. And the oft stagnant church of today continues in its cesspools of harbored resentments and bitterness, making very little positive impact on our post-Christian culture.

Forgiving has come in vogue in secular psychology. "Holding on to hurts and nursing grudges wears you down physically and emotionally," says Stanford University psychologist Fred Luskin. "**Forgiving someone can be a powerful antidote**," says the author of Forgive for Good.

> Secular psychology is cashing in on the benefits of forgiving.

Carl Thoresen, another Stanford University psychologist, formulated a six-session group treatment plan to help people forgive. His study indicates that the 259 adults who participated saw stress, anger and physical symptoms (like headaches and stomach upsets) diminish. Positive effects were reported to have remained six months later.

81

Forgiving defined

God has blessed me with two wonderful women as wives. Theresa is my current wife as of December, 2000. For 36 years, Ann was my first wife. Before the Lord propelled her into His presence through a brain aneurysm, she defined forgiving as,

<u>"I bear the reality of the hurt; then,</u>
<u>I choose to hold it against him/her no longer."</u>

The person who forgives faces completely the extent of hurt or wrong dealt to him

He doesn't rationalize.

He doesn't block it out of his mind, trying to forget it.

He doesn't cover or mask it with alcohol, drugs, shock treatments, or a lifestyle of busyness.

He faces the pain. Feels it. And he sets the offender free from the wrong. He wipes the slate clean.

Luskin comments:

"Forgiving isn't about condoning what happened.
It's about breaking free of the person who wronged us."

While dialoging with a client about forgiving, she interrupted me with, "Just a minute. There is no way I can forgive my stepfather. I wish God would burn him in hell, and before he does, I hope he will do everything to him that he did to me. I can't pick up a coat hanger without remembering the times he **beat me with hangers**. I can't touch water to my face without remembering the times he **held my head under water** until I would submit to his cruel sexual advances.

"Forgive him? You've got to be kidding! I want him to be **displayed in pornography** like he did me. I want him to experience the **sexual brutality** he gave me that even now prohibits me from bearing children.

82

"I want his **teeth broken off** at the roots by a phone being smashed into his face like he did to me... **tied to a bed** with **scalding water** thrown on him ... taken to the woods to **stand naked** for hours ... **burnt with cigarettes** ... **pushed down the stairs** ... kept prisoner in his own house for ten years without a friend .. (and more that is too cruel and lewd to mention here) ... like he did me! How can I but hate him?

"I want him to experience what I am going through now: the overwhelming **fears, depression, panic attacks, loss of memory, nightmares**. I want a psychiatrist to tell him he'll have to spend weeks in a mental hospital. And you say I have to forgive him? **He deserves more that the seven years in prison he got! He deserves hell!**"

Suppose you are the counselor. What would your reactions be? Part of me wanted to weep for the hurt Gail has experienced. Part of me wanted to strangle that "animal" stepfather. Yet, God says,

Vengeance is mine. I will repay.

My vengeance would be puny and weak compared to God's. Consider how God repays evil described in Isaiah 25:10-11

> *The hand of the LORD will rest on this mountain; but Moab will be trampled under him as straw is trampled down in the manure. They will spread out their hands in it, as a swimmer spreads out his hands to swim. God will bring down their pride despite the cleverness of their hands.*

| Horse |
| Manure: |
| God's |
| Vengeance? |

Now dear reader, I've mucked horse stalls, standing in manure and shavings with rubber boots. Think of what it would be like to be trampled under foot of horses in a manure pile so deep it was like you were swimming in it. Let your imagination run with that picture. "Vengeance is mine," says the Lord, "I will repay."

Besides praying that God would empower Gail to do the impossible and let God have the vengeance, I thought it necessary to address how **an unforgiving spirit harms us**. I related to her how an unforgiving spirit:

- is like an addiction. It has control over us like prison bars to an inmate, enslaving us to the past, keeping the wound open;
- does make one feel better immediately (by thinking vengefully), but it destroys in the long run, because it produces bitterness, which like an infection, effects us and those with whom we come in contact;
- freezes us into the offended time frame, locks us into what we resent and an area of emotional growth stops.

For example, the 14 year-old boy who angrily retorts: "I'm never going to let a woman dominate me like Mom does." That resentful statement locks him into that 14 year-old mind set. A powerful and substantial amount of emotional energy is focused on the offensive time and offender. He becomes emotionally enslaved. Emotional growth in that area stops and his relationship with women is forever stilted.

Or, the 17 year-old gal who resents her alcoholic father often finds herself at age 35 married to an alcoholic husband. **An unforgiving spirit locks us into that which we resent.**

An unforgiving spirit also:

- **hinders our fellowship** with God and others;
- **is the cause of a host** of physical, mental, emotional, spiritual and relational torment. Jesus describes it in a parable found in Matthew 18:21-35. It is the story of the unforgiving servant whose destination was life with the tormentors.
- **opens the door to satan.** 2 Corinthians 2:10-11
  If you forgive anyone, I also forgive him. And what I have forgiven—if there was anything to forgive—I have forgiven in the sight of Christ for your sake, in order that Satan might not outwit us. For we are not unaware of his schemes.
- **creates a self absorption.** Every life event gets processed through the eyes of bitterness which magnifies every little hurt and wrong - creating more self-centeredness.

"Gail," I said. "I don't blame you for not wanting to forgive him, but for your sake, for your own benefit, I hope you will allow God to begin His forgiving process through you to that cruel man."

Forgiving is not

As we scrutinize this topic, let's look first at what forgiving is not:

1. **Condemning** - "Oh, you want me to blame my parents for..." is often the initial response to exploring sources of emotional pain. The counselor's reply: "No we're not here to blame anyone, but to face realistically what happened and what your response has been." We assign responsibility - theirs and ours.

2. **Condoning\intellectualizing** (admitting an action was wrong but downplaying its destructiveness). "Dad beat me but his dad beat him worse than what I got."

3. **Denial** - trying to forget. "Ah, no big deal. Other people have it worse. Forget it."

4. **Reconciliation** - is not forgiving. They are two separate issues that we explored in the last chapter.

Forgiving is not placing blame, not condoning or denying. It is not necessarily reconciliation.

Forgiving is

> I cancel a debt that is real and treacherous.
> Mercy is extended to the offender.
> Justice is left up to God, because
> He says vengeance is His, He will repay.

Forgiving is vital to the healing of the inflicted wound. Complete healing comes through the destruction of any self-protective defenses (that we've just described in what forgiving is not) and a deep forgiving that depends on changing the rational, visual and emotional parts of the mind. We'll emphasize this later.

Forgiving is a process that begins with:

1. Disclosure\awareness.

I find that many people don't realize that they are carrying an unforgiving attitude. Thus, disclosure begins with praying the prayer of Psalm 139:23-4 Search me O God...

Counseling procedures we use with this prayer involve writing - either a **negative autobiography or making a list.**

> The <u>autobiography</u> involves walking back through memories in five year segments, asking God to help recall events that caused hurt, anger and guilt. Hurt and anger from those who have hurt you. Guilt from pain that you have caused others.

Write a sentence or two about the circumstances and what your response was. Too much detail written can lead to a verbal escape. Verbosity can cover up pain. Just a simple: "Dad wasn't there for me. That made me feel unwanted. It hurts."

Think through the last five years. Write. Move back to the previous five years and on back to earliest memories. **Very few adhere to the discipline this takes. Those who do experience great freedom.**

> Rather than a negative autobiography, some prefer making a <u>two-column list</u>: who hurt me or who did I hurt, and what were the circumstances. This **defines assignment of responsibility.**

Writing has a way of clarifying and making more real what happened. This is so important in the forgiving process because just a rational, thinking approach to forgiving tends to be an exercise with shallow results.

Bring a memory to recall. Identify the thoughts regarding the hurt. What **image** occurs? What happens as you dwell on the image? What **emotions** are triggered? Associate your memory with emotion. Hurt, rage, loss, grief, guilt?

Caution: dwell only long enough on the image to touch the pain. **If pain is dwelt on it can easily become an obsession** that becomes an escape from entering active forgiving. Rather than forgiving, the focus is the pain.

Examine defenses that have protected you from that pain - revenge, stuffing, withdrawing, anesthesia cover-up,

| No Pain, No Gain. |

rationalizing\spiritualizing, denial, shallow forgiving. Examine how they have protected you from the pain and obstructed the forgiving process. We're talking **about revisiting the event to produce the deepest healing.** (Christ set the example in his teaching. He often taught in word pictures that illicited not only a <u>rational</u> but also an <u>emotional</u> response.)

Make journaling in this manner an aggressive exercise:
- √ in your **daily formal discipline of solitude** with God; and,
- √ **spontaneously throughout the day.**
- √ **Integrate the memories** into self concept and how it affects it any other areas of your present life.
- √ **Tie the memory** to mental pictures, other emotions, other memories and ongoing events and people.
- √ **Ask God to reveal how bitterness impacts your everyday life**.

For example, a friend of mine found himself getting outrageously angry at his new wife whenever she would give him the slightest criticism. He exploded one day with, "If it weren't for you I could be a good Christian." He had not dealt with a burning anger toward his very dominating, critical mother. His overreactions toward his wife were mother-anger spilling out on his bride. A displacement that hurt his marriage.

He had to go through the mental pictures (images, memories and feelings) of his relationship with his mother, not to blame her but to acknowledge the root of his 'wife-anger" and deeply forgive his mother.

His strictly rational approach to forgiving would never take away the destructive power of an unforgiving spirit.

From an awareness of what needs forgiving, we move to the next step.

2. Desire to forgive

Forgiving is not natural, especially with the deep hurts inflicted by someone significant to us - a relative or a close friend. But God is in the business of changing lives and will soften our heart to help us want to forgive. Phillipians 2:13

> *for it is God who works in you to will and*
> *to act according to his good purpose.*

We might pray:

"Father, I know it is your good purpose for me to forgive, however, that hurt is so deep. I don't want to forgive. **I'd rather get even or withdraw** from the person. You must give me the desire to want to forgive. Thank you that you will."

This is where the Christian has an "edge" on the non-believer. A Christian has the Holy Spirit residing within, empowering toward obedience. The non-believer only has his will to mentally forgive. It would be like comparing dyeing a cloth to spray painting it. Dyeing permeates the entire body of the cloth (spiritual, mental forgiving). Painting it covers just the surface (mental forgiving only).

| DYE VERSUS SPRAY PAINT |

To help ourselves with the desire to forgive, it is appropriate to see how much God has forgiven us, because **our capacity to forgive is rooted in His forgiveness of us.** This is difficult to see in today's society because we hear very little teaching on the holiness of God verses the sinfulness of man. Sin and repentance are not themes preached in most pulpits. We even hide our depravity from ourselves.

Our challenge:

First, view God. **See his holiness and awesome power**. As in Psalm 97:1-6;

The LORD reigns, let the earth be glad; let the distant shores rejoice. Clouds and thick darkness surround him; righteousness and justice are the foundation of his throne. Fire goes before him and consumes his foes on every side. His lightning lights up the world; the earth sees and trembles. The mountains melt like wax before the LORD, before the Lord of all the earth. The heavens proclaim his righteousness, and all the peoples see his glory.

Isaiah beheld God as seen in Isaiah chapter 6. And his response was "woe is me..."

We get a glimpse of God and our response should be:
"I see your awesome holiness contrasted by my unholiness (my idolatry, harsh critical spirit, lust, greed, laziness, pride, my lack of faith, critical spirit.) Thank you for forgiving me. Thus, who am I not to forgive when I have received so much forgiveness myself?"

In Matthew 6:15 we find:
But if you do not forgive men their sins, your Father will not forgive your sins.

My interpretation:
if I don't forgive someone's sin against me,
I won't sense God's forgiveness of my sins.

If I find a person who is still wrestling with the desire to forgive, a couple suggestions are offered.

1. **Endeavor to sense the neediness of the person who hurt you.** People who hurt, hurt people. To discern his pain can soften your heart to want to forgive him for the pain he inflicted on you.

> People who hurt, hurt people.

Caution: don't do this too quickly in the forgiving process, lest

89

it become a rationalizing tool to avoid facing pain. Make sure your own anguish has been thoroughly felt before seeing the offender's pain.

2. **Distinguish the value of the inflicted pain in your own life.** If according to Romans 8:28, everything is to work out for our good, then asking God how He wants to use the pain as some good gift will help transform the resentful

> What you meant for evil, God planned for good.

focus toward the offender. As Joseph said to his cruel brothers: "what you meant for evil, God planned for good." **This brings a change in focus toward the offender.**

The forgiving process begins with disclosure\awareness - an honesty with oneself about wounds that may still be unhealed. Forgiving continues with a prayerful spirit that requests God to create the desire to forgive. And now we look at the word "decision". **Disclosure - desire - decision.**

3. Decision
Paul emphasizes forgiving in Ephesians 4:31-32
> *Stop being mean, bad-tempered and angry. Quarreling,*
> *harsh words, and dislike of others should have no*
> *place in your lives. Instead, be kind to each other,*
> *tenderhearted, <u>forgiving one another</u>, just as God has*
> *forgiven you because you belong to Christ.*

While step 2 is a prayer for desire to forgive, step 3 is decision. An act of the will. The feeling to want to forgive may still not be very strong but a decision is made: "I choose to hold it against him no longer. I wipe his slate clean."

Recall that forgiving is allowing the painful scene to unfold in your mind (**envision**), feeling the devastation of it (**emotions**) then choosing to forgive (**rationality**).

90

The process is like placing the hurtful memory in a package and situating it in a hot air balloon. The balloon is anchored to the ground with scores of rope moorings. Every time the forgiving process is identified (hopefully daily) another mooring is cut loose. **The deeper the hurt, the greater the number of moorings.** Each loosened mooring prepares the balloon for its flight into freedom.

Forgiveness
in a balloon

What will this freedom feel like? Look like? **The memory may remain but in a transformed state.** The focal point will not be the painful event but the value, the benefit personally from the painful circumstance. **Gratitude will be the focus**, not the resentment. *Gratitude, not so much for what happened, but for how God has or is using the wounding in your life in a positive way for yourself and others.*

Some would say there may always be some pain when the memory is relived. My counseling experience is that in complete forgiveness the pain is gone. However, the question is probably irrelevant because the issue is: when I've allowed God to complete his forgiveness work in me toward that offender, my response to the hurtful memory is "thanks," because the memory is transformed into an image of value to me. **The story has been rewritten from victim to hero.**

As a 12 year old I was **sexually molested** by a camp counselor. He was a very nurturing man - in fact he became a father figure to me over the 6-week camping period. But he contaminated it with sexual acts. I didn't realize the negative impact of it all until years later when I saw how what he had affected my sexual relationship with my wife. A seething rage brewed within me.

However, the forgiving process lead me to a **transformed image** of what he did. I saw how God used it to create in me a greater need for Him and <u>His</u> nurturing of me. I felt a greater sensitivity toward meeting my wife's needs. It also emphasized to me the great need to <u>appropriately</u> nurture boys and men with whom I come in contact. It gave me a greater compassion for homosexuals whose lifestyle often begins with such an encounter.

The anger is gone.
The molestation memory remains,
but in a transformed state.

Caution: you may think that the balloon has been completely set free, when months or even years later an aching reoccurs.

"Oh, no, I thought I had dealt with that. Does this mean I haven't forgiven at all?"

No. It seems that there are situations where God says, "I'll give you as much awareness of an excruciating event as I know you can handle (I Corinthians 10:13). You and I will work on forgiving and later I'll make you aware of a deeper level of anguish. We'll continue the forgiving process at a deeper level."

FORGIVE! Jesus commands it, Paul emphasizes it and looking at ourselves selfishly, **it's good for us**. The other person might not deserve your forgiving - but you do. So much of what we see in the counseling office - depression, anxiety, family problems and more is tied so closely to an unforgiving, vengeful spirit. As a Chinese proverb suggests: One who pursues revenge should dig two graves.

> One who pursues revenge should dig two graves.

For your own mental, emotional, physical,
spiritual and relational freedom - forgive.

You might not have an experience like Gail, but let's make sure the forgiving of your situation is complete. So complete that you can pray for a heart of love for the offender - love that may need boundaries to prevent further abuse. Which leads us to the next concern: reconciliation.

4. Reconciliation?

Romans 12:18 tells us:

> *If it is possible, as far as it depends on you,*
> *live at peace with everyone.*

"If I forgive, do I need to restore relationship with the offender?"

Reconciliation is often a question asked in fear because the one who committed the offensive act(s) was a parent. Reconciliation could place you back in a position of repeat abuse or if grandchildren are involved, they could be mistreated.

Forgiveness and reconciliation are two different issues.

We're not obligated to trust an adversary with reconciliation, but we are compelled to forgive!

Reconciliation depends on the offender

1. renouncing his previous hurtful action,
2. repenting, and
3. taking steps to insure that it will unlikely happen again.

> Requirements for Reconciliation

With a repentant spirit and obvious remedial activity, the offender builds back trust slowly for reconciliation to take place. The remedial activity could be long term counseling, accountability with a group, active pursuit of growth through study, church, workshops, etc.

In this manner the one offended will be receptive to reconciliation as the forgiveness process is completed. Luke 17:3 says *If he repents, forgive him* ... This does not mean we forgive only if an offender repents. It means that

for restoration of relationship, the offender must demonstrate a repentant attitude and behavior.

Without this, reconciliation is not possible.

How true this is even in marriage. Abuse may continue. A forgiving spirit must remain cultivated toward the offender, but that doesn't mean the offended lays down and takes a doormat, eat carpet position. Physical or extreme emotional abuse must not continue. There are options for the offended.

Matthew 18:15-18 gives direction. **Confrontation is first personal**. No satisfactory results? Take at least one other with you. No satisfactory results? The church is then instructed to be brought into the relationship action.

There is an African-American church in Los Angeles that interprets the Matthew 18 passage this way. The pastor described it, "If a woman comes to a leader of our church with a complaint

> If not
> reconciliation,
> then what?

regarding physical abuse from her husband, the man is confronted and warned that if abuse happens again, four men will pay him a not so kindly visit that will definitely curtail his desire to abuse again."

Separation, to prevent the continued abuse, may be another option.

Forgiveness and reconciliation are not necessarily synonymous!

Another facet of the forgiving process can not be overlooked.

5. Repentance

Disclosure, desire, decision is followed by repentance.

Of What? "I wasn't the scoundrel, the abusive parent, the cruel friend, the abandoning spouse. For what do I need to repent?"

I need to repent for my resentful response. My bitterness. My revenge. My coping strategies. The pain I've caused others. Matthew 6:12

Forgive us our debts, as we also have forgiven our debtors.

Notice the sequence: forgive to be forgiven.

God's forgiveness of my sins removes any guilt on my part. Isaiah 1:18 LB:

Come, let's talk this over says the Lord;
no matter how deep the stain of your sins,
I can take it out and make you as clean
as freshly fallen snow. Even if you are stained
as red as crimson, I can make you white as wool.
No guilt!

In summary:
Forgiving
1   is one of the **most difficult challenges** we'll pursue, requiring an aggressive, daily commitment;
2. is **commanded by Jesus** and empowered by Him (Matthew 6:15);
3. is **not** **condoning, rationalizing**, denying or avoiding;
4. **involves the whole person** - visual, emotional, rational, spiritual, memory, morality, ethics, willing to see our own need for forgiveness and understanding of and desire for right relationships;
5. **transforms focus** from the offender's inflicted pain to how God has used the wound as a source of value - a benefit;
6. slowly **transforms our character** to the image of Christ;
7. is an **ongoing process** the rest of our lives.

Gail
I must finish the story of Gail. Her symptoms grew worse. She became a prisoner in her own home, except when she went out for a jog, which was part of my prescription for depression.

On a fateful Tuesday, she became so disoriented while jogging that she lost her way. She had to stop a passerby to ask where she lived. To her chagrin, the person pointed to her house just three houses away.

She called me in a tremendous depression. My words to her were that the distortion of memory, the depression, the weird thinking were mostly tied to the hate for her stepfather.

| If all else fails - pray! |

"Gail," I challenged, "even if you need to go to a church group and request prayer support, do it. You must let go of all of that hate. Possibly a group praying for you would help you let go of it and replace it with a forgiving, loving attitude."

That was around one o'clock in the afternoon. At about five o'clock, I received a call from Gail saying, "Dr. Burwick, I'm free!" In Gail's words, "something just had to happen. I am a Christian, and I shouldn't have to be going through this. If this is related to the hatred for my stepfather, I had better resolve it. I've begun to forgive."

She called her stepfather who lived in a country across the globe.

She relates: "I was scared to death. What would I hear on the other end of the line? Would I receive a blast of dirty profanity? I said, 'hello, Jim, this is Gail'. He very nearly came through the phone.

"Oh Gail. It is so good to hear you. I've spent thousands of dollars on private investigators, trying to locate you. I've become a Christian and I do so much need you to forgive me for the terrible way I treated you. I'll do anything. My weekly paycheck is yours for the rest of my life if that would bring about your forgiveness."

"Ray, he was in tears," she said. "As we talked, it seemed as if a dark, oppressing cloud lifted from me. We hung up, and immediately I saw a coat hangar in my room. I could pick up that hangar without the terrible memories reappearing of the scores of times he had beaten me with a coat hangar. Tonight I'm going to take my first bath in 17 years." (She had showered, but hadn't been able to bathe because of the memories of being held under water until she would yield to his cruel, selfish demands.) I went to the shopping center and could ride an escalator without holding on for dear life. My loss of memory is minimal. I'm free!"

Freedom. She thought. However, she was so overwhelmed by the hatred toward her stepfather that she was unaware of the subtle resentments building within her towards her neighbors, her work, her husband and various other targets.

We don't just carry a bitterness toward one person. It spills out and touches others.

It took Gail some time even to admit to and then face the large reservoir of anger within.

The following weeks were tumultuous. Along with the tremendous reservoir of anger, she became aware of her need to control and dominate those around her. She saw her great desire for attention as she would pour out her troubles to anyone who would listen. She rebelled against her husband's leadership. She saw her wanton waste of money. It was all difficult to face.

There were days when she would plead for escape - to the hospital, to wherever. There were times when she would blame everyone else, and her mind would again become disoriented. There were days she would label, "the greatest I have lived. I see all my hate, my irresponsibility and my rebellion. I'm letting go, allowing the Lord to have them. He is changing me."

As these better days became more frequent, her symptoms dissipated, antidepressants and tranquilizers were phased out, and she became a vibrant testimony for Christ.

Not all my clients have such a dramatic story and for some, reconciliation never occurs because the offender is unrepentant. But, no matter what the offender's response, we must forgive for our own sake!

Anyone you need to forgive?
Forgive us our debts, as we also have forgiven our debtors. More on forgiving in the next chapter.

Scripture:
Romans 12:18: *If it is possible, as far as it depends on you, live at peace with everyone.*

Prayer:
Father, show me if there is someone to whom I've not finished the forgiving process.

Exercise:
The greatest wound I have experienced:
From my parents: _____

From my children (if applicable) _____

From peers: _____

From performance (school, athletics, music, etc) _____
_____

From a spouse: _____

From another authority figure (pastor, coach, teacher, boss, etc) _____
_____

To my ego: _____

Any more Facing - Feeling - Forgiving needed?
Suggested reading: <u>To Forgive is Human</u>, McCullough, Sandage, Worthington

Have I <u>Really</u> Forgiven?
A Checklist to Help Determine

✓ Did a significant person in my early life fail to give me the nurturing I needed? Were my emotional needs neglected?

✓ Has someone I trusted been disloyal to me and betrayed my trust?

✓ Do I find myself dwelling on an offense — a hurtful situation often coming to mind?

✓ When I think of a person, does his failure toward me often come to mind?

✓ Do I have a free-floating anger or bitterness which spills over to unrelated situations where I overreact toward others?

✓ Do I find myself rationalizing for someone who has hurt me by saying, "He didn't mean it," or "He was treated the same way," or "She didn't know any better?"

✓ Do I describe my parents as "perfect" or my childhood as ideal?

✓ Am I waiting for an apology or repentance to begin forgiving someone who has sinned against me?

✓ When someone hurts me, do I just "put it out of my mind?"

✓ Things in my life have not been great but I just look at how much worse off others are.

✓ I am unable to see any good come from my pain and wonder how God could have possibly allowed it.

Because forgiving is commanded by God, and because an unforgiving spirit (conscious or unconscious) is so destructive, consider using the above as a prayer meditation, asking God to reveal any resentment that you may still carry. Journaling insights is helpful.

Nine

Release

More On Forgiving- A Tale of Two Wives

"The world has no rage like love to hatred turned,
not hell a fury like a woman scorned."

Two Christian colleges have designated scholarships in memory of my first wife, Ann. I think it appropriate for me to **continue her legacy through the following material.** Though I am extremely happy in my current marriage to Theresa, Ann was a significant part of my life for 36 years. Much of what I've learned, she and I learned together, sometimes because of each other. Sometimes in spite of each other! (All marriages have challenges, some more severe then others.)

She gave me permission to write part of her story in the first book on anger. I continue that now as an example of how forgiving can bring such great freedom. **May Ann's legacy be expanded through your encounter with her "anger report."**

ANN'S UNIQUE STORY

Ann is a classic example of a person with unrecognized, pent-up resentment displaying itself in a **mind of turmoil.** In her early 30's, although walking in fellowship with the Lord, she began to experience **unusual thinking patterns,** such as false guilt and irrational fears - fear of losing control mentally, of insanity, fear of being alone. Other fears that are too personal to share.

She didn't want me to go to work, wanted me there beside her all the time. She had a guilt-induced compulsion to confess for anything. If she stepped on an ant, she had to confess that as sin. If she used a metal spatula on someone else's Teflon pan, that was a tormenting sin that had to be confessed over and over.

The **confession obsession** came after we visited with our pastor, who in his lack of knowledge, told her to just confess her sins and all 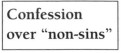 guilt would be gone. Neither she nor I knew of any sin she was carrying, hence the confession over "non-sins".

Confession over "non-sins"

Ann went through hours of deep introspection, trying to sort out the fears, the reality of them and the possible cause. At times she felt as if she were **outside of her body seeing herself** and others from a distance. She seemed to be losing her mind, and I feared for her life. In fact, she often said, "**Ray, just commit me to the mental institution so I won't hurt anyone.**"

As <u>desperation and despair increased</u>, God used Dr. Henry Brandt, a Christian psychologist and author of many books, to show us God's answer. Dr. Brandt unselfishly and graciously agreed to meet us at the Seattle, Washington airport, he arriving from the north; we from the east. The three-hour counseling encounter began.

Before long, Dr. Brandt was lovingly, gently, yet firmly saying, "Ann, you have much bitterness within you." She denied it. I denied it. **How could such a loving, super-sweet person be filled with bitterness?**

Before the session ended, Ann began to catch a glimpse of the **pent-up anger**. Dr. Brandt told her to confess it whether or not it was apparent and to ask God to cleanse her angry spirit.

We left the airport excited that there was an answer and very grateful to Dr. Brandt. But we in no way realized that the next three years would be marked by trauma and pain, resulting in a tremendously purifying experience that would see God remaking both Ann and me.

Jeremiah wrote,
I did as he told me, and found the potter working at his wheel.
But the jar that he was forming didn't turn out as he wished,
so he kneaded it into a lump and started again. Then the Lord said:

O Israel (Ray and Ann), can't I do to you as this potter has done to this clay? As the clay is in the potter's hand, so are you in my hand.
(Chapter 18:3-6 TLB).

Though we both desired to walk closely with God, **we didn't realize how much reforming the potter had to do with us.**

Ann's symptoms of <u>weird thinking began to disappear quite rapidly</u>.

* She studied positive Scripture daily.
* Introspection was curtailed.
* She gave more of herself to others.
* When a weird thought or fear would come to mind she would pray, **"Lord, I know what I am thinking is not true, although it certainly seems to be. By faith in Dr. Brandt's counsel, I believe this is a cover-up for pent-up anger. I don't even feel my anger now, God, but I confess it to you as the cause of this symptom. God, take my angry spirit. Love and forgive through me."**

> Symptoms gone, but deep anger surfaced.

Within two weeks, most of the symptoms were gone. However, the deep anger that had been lying dormant for years began to surface. Because of my insecurity, I began to be very reactive, threatened and angry. **My inner ugliness surfaced.** Oh, the pain and trauma that ensued within and between both of us.

C.S. Lewis said,

> **"God <u>whispers</u> to us in our pleasures.**
> *He <u>speaks</u> to us through our conscience,*
> *and <u>shouts</u> at us in our pain.*
> **Pain is God's megaphone to arouse a deaf world."**

God was gently shouting at us, getting us ready for our next encounter with a godly man who would share further truth with us.

Two and a half years after God blessed us with Dr.Brandt's visit, we encountered Dr. Charles Solomon. Through his teaching we began to learn the dynamic concept of not only seeing our sin, but **being aware of the underlying sin nature - the self.**

> The wounds and self-centeredness that
> under lied most of our anger.

He shared with us the concept of co-death, co-resurrection with Christ. **That we live now with the power of the Creator alive in us. That He provides the power and the healing to address these life issues (that everyone has) to provide wholeness and peace.**

Ann's "mind in turmoil" was caused by unrecognized pent-up anger that lead to an unforgiving spirit. As she learned to face the wounds of the past and her subsequent anger, she proceeded with the forgiving process toward me and others who had wronged her. She claimed her position in Christ and her mind became one of peace and strength. (This concept is explained in more detail in chapter 12.)

Ann's life of productivity

Paul wrote,

> *For God has not given us the spirit of fear;*
> *but of power, and of love, and of a sound mind.*
> (2 Timothy 1:7).

Ann went on to live a life of great productivity, counseling hundreds of women into greater wholeness. Scores and scores of condolence notes after her death at the age of 58, witnessed to her effectiveness in loving people and helping them in their journey to wholeness and peace. I am a very blessed man to have partnered with her for 36 years and her children have a great heritage because of her.

THERESA'S UNIQUE STORY

As of this writing, Theresa and I have been married nearly 6 years. What a wonderful gift from God. She too, has had her emotional challenges. **Panic attacks ruled her life** for years. For graduate school she had to commute an hour and a half to Portland State University (if she took the freeway). But freeways presented greater opportunity for panic, so back roads were taken, meaning a much longer commute.

She described her challenge this way:

"Last night a situation triggered memories. I emotionally went back to the time when I began having the **panic attacks**, lots of **acid reflux**, and probably a very <u>damaged esophagus.</u> It would spasm when I drank anything but a tepid beverage. Many foods would cause the acid reflux to flare. **My body became my adversary**. I would sit in my chair and try to distance myself from the fear. Some nights I would go do bed and **wonder if I'd live through the night.**

"I could only cry out to God and leave my life in His hands. I would try to become still and wait for the physical turmoil to pass. It was very scary, yet a time of growing quietness, of **turning to God in a desperate way** and **finding Him a comforting friend.**

"I never had much communication with my dad, but of what we had, probably 80% was critical, often spoken

| Conflict in significant relationships |

sharply to my retreating back. 'You are the most rude, impudent girl in Albany!' was flung at me as I stomped my way upstairs to my bedroom. There were never visits, casual conversations. I suppose the most time we were ever in the same area was in the car going back and forth to church. Maybe I've forgotten some good times.

"Previous marriages have not gone well. There were times best described as

a swirl of black, angry storm clouds around my head, filling the atmosphere with harshness, blackness.
As I think about it now, I have the urge to escape.

"I had allowed myself to slip into an **intellectual approach**

to handling my feelings of hurt and anger. It was my fault for their imperfections. In my care-taking mode, I assumed responsibility."

In the last couple years, Theresa has begun facing the pain within, taking responsibility for her reactions of hurt and anger. Besides facing the anger toward many sources, she is claiming God's power to **forgive through her** at an ever deepening level. She is also handling it with her bright mind:

> **"God is my resource, my strong tower, my champion. If He says I'm safe, I'm safe! If He says He equips me for battle, He does. I do not need to be a punching bag. I don't need to do irrational things. I have a voice, a mind; I can speak when I need to. I do not ever need to be overcome with fear! A part of me has never taken advantage of God's protection, never accessed it, especially in times of danger: emotional, verbal, physical or otherwise."**

Panic attacks are gone. Esophagus is healed. Fears are minimized at worst, gone at best.

> Forgiving
> Process
> Completed

Recall with me - one of the signs of completion of the forgiving process is the ability to give thanks for the pain. It sounds something like:

> "I've so deeply walked through the pain. So plugged into God's resources to forgive you that I can now see how God will use (or is using) the pain you put me through for my good and His glory. What you did was wrong, but I'm thankful to God for the results He has and is accomplishing."

All parents make mistakes. I could write a book about mine and my children could write numerous books about my blunders as a parent. I was once very resentful toward my parents for mistakes they made in child rearing that helped to formulate a **grotesque stuttering speech** pattern in me.

I had <u>terrible fears of speaking</u>. I often got hung up on a word and could not say it, once even **dislocating my jaw trying to say a word**. When I was on the basketball coaching staff with Athletes in Action, a taped basketball TV show had to be canceled because my stuttering ruined the presentation (days before Mel Tillis!). **Tears of embarrassment and anger often streaked my cheeks.**

But now I would not change it for the world, even if I could do it all over again and be free of stuttering. The product **of stuttering** has been:

- A deeper **dependency on the Holy Spirit** even to be able to speak.
- An ever intensifying awareness of my **need for intimacy with "Abba Papa."**
- A keen **ability to listen** (can't talk when you stutter, gotta listen.)
- A developed **empathy for hurting people** and a desire to help them. I became an effective counselor in part because of stuttering.
- And a lot of **character growth** that if I enumerate, I'll get cocky and ruin the whole process.

After working through the forgiving process with my parents, I can say, **"Thank you, God, for my stuttering. Thank you, Dad and Mom, for your strengths and for the weaknesses that played a part in the cause of my stuttering."**

I wasted a lot of energy and suffered much discomfort because of all that resentment that I carried (mostly unknowingly) for years. James 1:2-4 tells us:

Consider it pure joy, my brothers, whenever you face trials of many kinds, because you know that the testing of your faith develops perseverance. Perseverance must finish its work so that you may be mature and complete, not lacking anything.

As you and I forgive others for pain they have caused us, the spirit of God builds in us strong character until we are "mature and complete." Our gratitude turns to praise, and praise is the great decentralizer of self.

Getting eyes off self and circumstances and onto God and to others alleviates much personal discomfort.

The **process of forgiveness is terminated** as we let go of the offense and can pray that God would richly bless the offender. We look for ways to express love to that person, not expecting anything in return.

I wish I could say that all of my clients leave the counseling office free from paranoia, physical symptoms, weird thinking, anxiety, marital hang-ups, stuttering and depression.

> **Not all people become free**

Some obviously want to continue hanging onto and hugging the hurts, **drinking the poison of bitterness at their solitary pity-party.** With others, I've not been effective because of my tendency to try to rush in and fix it, causing the counseling process to abort.

But words cannot express the joy and fulfillment I feel when I walk through the **fiery furnace of hurts and hates** with a client and see them allow God to bring them out **unscathed.** In fact, they appear from the furnace stronger people, with the only indication of burning being the absence of fetters of fears, insecurities, resentments and guilt. Only these fetters that bound them were inflamed.

Many more stories could be printed here. A question challenges us:

If God forgave us for all our sins, who are we not to forgive those who sin against us?

Scripture:

Romans 8:28-29 *And we know that* **in all things God works for the good of those who love him, who have been called according to his purpose.** *For those God foreknew he also predestined to be conformed to the likeness of his Son...*

Exercise:

As the Holy Spirit brings back to recall wounds in your past, are any **not meeting the forgiving criteria of giving thanks?** Remember, it is not thanks for the wound, but for how God has or is using the wound for your good and His glory.

_____

_____

Which of the wounds of the past can you see are resulting in your good and God's glory?_____

_____

_____

Prayer:

Father, I want to follow your injunction to "give thanks in all things." Please give me insight on my progress. I don't want to too quickly "give thanks" lest that be a spiritualized defense mechanism to cover the pain. Nor do I want it to be a flippant "obedience." Empower me to so deeply work through the forgiving process that the conclusion is a focus on how you turned "evil" for good. Thank you, Father.

Ten

Tame the Wild Beast

Present Anger - Managed

Never go to bed mad. Stay up and fight. Phyllis Diller

The problem of **anger is so prolific** that over four million web sites can be found (at this writing) when "anger solution" is typed into one search engine.

Cities have **anger management classes** as part of disciplinarian measures for road rage and domestic abuse. Other institutions are addressing the anger problem that many people experience.

We live in an angry, explosive society. Can the "wild beast" be tamed? Managed? Is there something better then anger management? Your call. Check out these next two chapters and see what you think.

From many sources you'll find
anger management techniques:
1. <u>Cognate</u> (think).
Pay attention to what you think, what you do, what you feel

| Think |

when you are angry. Know what irritates you in different situations. Identify the cause of your anger so that you can decide what you will do with it. Check to see if your anger is signaling some other stress like fatigue, worry, hunger, loneliness or fear. The stress might be making you more susceptible to anger. Is the current situation reminding you of a hurtful past situation? Is this a situation where you are not getting your way?

2. Cognitive restructuring.

(Change the way you think.) The National Mental Health Association states:

"Logic defeats anger, because anger, even when it is justified, can quickly become_ irrational, very exaggerated and overly_ dramatic."

Irrational accusations are a byproduct.

When angry, people tend to think in exaggerated terms.

- **Avoid negative words** like "you never... you always... I hate."
- View the situation from **another angle.**
- **What is positive** in the situation?
- **What can I learn** from it?
- Was this a **real threat or imagined?**
- Am I hearing the **other person's heart?**
- Is there **miscommunication?**

> Think
> Differently

3. Deep breathing

This is one of the most common suggestions for anger management. This technique probably has two components. The deep breathing

- distracts from the anger focus and it also
- releases some of the body's tension from anger. (Chest breathing doesn't have the relaxation effect that breathing from your "gut" produces.)

4. Repetition of calming words, comforting phrases.

Instead of "I hate him", think "I am angry with him, but I can deal with this. **There is a solution. Good can come out of this."**

5. Imagery.

Plan ahead for a visualization that is calming. **Visualize** lying on a warm, sandy beach, looking up at soft, fluffy clouds that are slowly passing overhead. (Admittedly, when I heard of this as an anger management technique, I snickered. I've never met a person, who with the initial outburst of anger, would switch gears so dramatically that knocking a person's block off could be so easily conformed to soft fluffy clouds. Maybe it is possible. Not with me.)

6. Exercise

releases physical energy that has been built up by anger. It **calms the mind and body**. Exercise doesn't get at the roots of the anger issue, but it provides a great outlet.

7. Perform a comforting or fulfilling task

Read a book. Clean up the house. Mow the lawn. Chop some firewood.

8. Problem solving.

Instead of focusing on the anger, center on **possible solutions** to the problem. "Is this my issue? Is this the other person's problem? How can this be discussed to bring resolution?

9. Listen

without defensiveness when criticized. **Learn**. You might be only one percent wrong in the conflict, the other person 99% off beam. **Learn** how your one percent can be corrected. **Listen** for the message that this person may feel neglected or unloved.

10. Speak "the truth in love."

Tell the other person in a non-attacking, rational, calm voice why you are angry and what would make you feel better. Some label this **assertive confrontation**. Be open to the other person's perspective.

11. Write the anger.

A journal or a letter to the person (usually unsent). **Be as angry as you want to be on paper.** If you're thinking cuss words, write them. Researcher James Pennebaker and others have demonstrated in well-designed experiments that writing about distressing experiences **reduces blood pressure, muscle tension, and visits to physicians for health reasons**. Journaling also produces better performance at school and work and improves immune function.

12. Humor diffuses.

Even laughing inwardly can tame the beast. We're not talking about sarcastic humor or laughing off your problems. Look to see if there can be any humor in the situation. You may humorously say inwardly, **"He looks like a pit bull when he's angry at me."**

13. Time out.

Ask for a moment to calm down. Leave the room. Take a potty break. Go for a walk and get some fresh air. Collect your thoughts and **come back to conflict resolution** within a reasonable time so that the issue is not avoided indefinitely.

14. A formal negotiation or mediation

may be necessary to resolve conflict. A third party can calm waters, hear both sides and suggest avenues to explore for resolution.

15. Avoid anger-inducing situations

This is hard to do if the major conflict is with your spouse. One anger-inducing situation in marriage is bedtime. Frequently, the male has skirted the marital conflict issue during the day. The **wife has a captive audience in bed**. Anger issues are tossed out. It's as if she is saying, "now I've got his attention. He can't get away. We are going to talk about that issue."

Of course, bedtime is not a productive time. People are tired and more easily say things in an exaggerated way. Besides, sleep is certainly affected.

Ann and I had a rule. If an anger issue was to be discussed at bedtime, we'd get up and go into the bathroom where there was no comfortable seating arrangement. Issues were discussed much more quickly or were completely avoided, because we wanted to avoid the bath "court room."

Taming The Other Person's Wild Beast

In taming the wild beast, we've looked at our own beast, but how do we tame someone else's? Can we? Is it possible? The following is a strategy <u>adapted</u> from an e-mail message. The source I have forgotten so can not give credit where it is due.

1. <u>Understand and agree</u>

If you truly understand why people are feeling angry in the first place, you will more easily know what to say and do (and what NOT to say or do) to tame their wild beast.

> find some way to agree

Whenever you are faced with an angry person, **find some way to agree** with whatever is upsetting them. Granted, this will be difficult to do at times. But the more you can agree with the ways the angry person is looking at the world, the more you will gain their confidence and give them the feeling of being heard.

You see, **angry people usually do have some valid points** to make. They are usually very good at spotting little things that you or others may have done wrong. And they often pick up on things you might have said or done of which you are unaware. This phenomenon can be very helpful for your own personal or relational growth.

The problem with angry people is that they don't want to see what THEY might have done wrong, or how THEY might have contributed to whatever misfortune has befallen them. Trying to point out the truth to angry individuals will only make the situation worse.

Thus, when you agree with whatever they do see (and which provoked their anger), you will be allowing the angry person to **help you focus on parts of the truth** that you may not have noticed or thought about previously.

At the very least, if you find it impossible to agree with any-

We are all selfish to some extent

thing the angry person is saying, you can always say something like, "I can understand how that would be upsetting," or "I would certainly be angry myself, if something like that happened to me." These statements let you agree with the person's emotions, even if you can't agree with any of the thoughts, assumptions, or perceptions that are fueling them.

The next time an angry loved one blasts you with a criticism like "You always think about your own needs while totally ignoring mine," just honestly say, **"You're right, I do tend to do that more than I should."**

However, a caution here. There are times when agreeing with an angry person **can cause more problems than it solves.** Obviously, you wouldn't want to agree wholeheartedly with untruthful, incriminating, destructive accusations.

2. <u>What an angry person wants</u>

Understanding what an angry person wants is critical:

1) They want you to **admit** that you did something very wrong;

2) They want you to acknowledge and **empathize with the pain and/or damage** you have caused them or others;

3) They want you to admit that you, and **you alone are 100% to blame** for whatever happened, and that they had little or nothing to do with it;

4) They want you to **take full responsibility by apologizing** for what you did wrong, by offering to make amends, or by being appropriately punished or sanctioned for your misdeeds.

**If angry people don't get this from you,
their anger will intensify.**

It really doesn't matter if one or more of the above listed assumptions/perceptions is not really true (which is usually the case). It might matter to you; but it matters very little to the person who is angry.

In general, angry people play the **victim role**, so focused on their internal feelings, opinions, and beliefs that they are not really open to seeing things any other way. In fact, if you try to point out any flaws in their thinking, it will only look (to them) like you are trying to avoid responsibility, and it will just make them more convinced their initial assumptions were correct!

> ANGRY
> VICTIMS

3. The challenge

Herein lies the crux of the challenge in dealing with angry people. **How do you get someone** who is looking at things incorrectly, or who has blown something minor way out of proportion, **to see things more correctly** without actually correcting them (since this will only make their anger worse)? The answer is often that **you can't**, at least not while they are in the throes of their anger.

Perhaps later, once they've settled down, they might be open to examining and correcting their mistaken assumptions. But in the heat of the moment, when people are very angry, only a few will be able to be this adaptable.

Remember, very few people are receptive to this strategy. Remember also that **you won't always have the calmness and presence of mind to apply these concepts when you are actively engaged with an angry individual.** But, the more you practice this strategy, and the more you practice remembering how angry people think and what angry people want, the better you will become at relating to them.

4. Don't defend or try to convince

A corollary to the principle above (always try to agree with angry people) is to avoid trying to defend yourself or trying to convince the angry person that you are not responsible for which they are accusing you. Elaborating on a former point, defending oneself when attacked, feeds the attacker's desire to attack more. Debating points of fact or arguing logically with angry people is only going to make matters worse.

> *They are not of the mind to let you win any of these debates. They are not going to be open minded to anything of a defensive or explanatory nature you might have to offer. Trying to defend yourself will only make the angry person more convinced you are guilty of serious wrong doings and are trying to wiggle off the hook.*

Always try to be in an understanding, listening, and helpful mode when interacting with angry individuals. **The more talking YOU do, the less likely a good outcome will be achieved.** The temptation will be great to try to defend yourself or to try to set the record straight, but you've got to resist this temptation early on in the game. Perhaps later, when you've won the confidence and trust of the other person and have defused much of their anger, you can try to make a few points and see what response you get.

5. Feel their pain

One of the best things you can do when confronted by an angry person is to just let them know you truly appreciate their pain. A key subconscious motive that drives people to become enraged is that they don't really believe other people will feel their pain (or agree with their point of view), so

> **they have to mount an exaggerated emotional outburst in order to get the attention they feel they deserve.**

All angry people want others to appreciate, sympathize with, and agree with how hurt, offended, betrayed, or disappointed they are feeling.

Once you have agreed with, empathized with, and let the angry person know you have heard their complaint and have felt their pain, it is **now time to take effective action**. At this point, you can try several things.

- You can try to reason with the person and attempt to correct any misperceptions they might have. This won't always work, as it depends a great deal on the maturity and open-mindedness of the other person.
- Another useful strategy is to apologize and offer to make amends for whatever part you may have played in the offense.

So, in endeavoring to tame another's wild beast, **responding appropriately can't be overemphasized.** I question whether it can be done in human strength. Our own wild beast doesn't like to succumb to or placate the wild beast in another. Is this not the place to apply 2 Corinthians 9:8?

> *"And God is able to make all grace abound to you, so that in all things at all times, having all that you need, you will abound in every good work."*

We certainly need God's grace to deal with an angry person.

Remember,

> angry people always want you to **understand their pain** and to admit **you did something wrong.** If they can't get that, they definitely want you to **apologize and offer to make amends.** Failure to do either of these two things will justify their anger even more.

You are not responsible for another person's anger, because you can't make another person angry. You can only bring out what is inside. However, you may help tame another's angry spirit by following the afore mentioned principles which are all wrapped up in Proverbs 15:1

A gentle answer turns away wrath,
but a harsh word stirs up anger.

Wrap-up

These and other anger management techniques can be garnered from books, workbooks, web sites, experience and other sources. How effective are they? How do they work for you?

Most of these do have merit. People are learning techniques to manage their anger more appropriately. I especially like the **journaling** concept. It gets my anger out where I'm not only expressing it but also clarifying issues for resolution. **Physical exercise** is also a must for me.

> Anger management is okay; however, there is a more productive way.

Along with these management concepts, I believe there is a more productive means to not just manage anger, but to see a lessening of its intensity and frequency.

As a young, aspiring basketball player, I had the privilege of attending a summer basketball camp sponsored by some of the Boston Celtics. What a great experience to hear **Bill Russell** talk of his psyche techniques on the opposition. To watch his blocking out strategy on the boards. To be taught by the leading professional free throw shooter at that time, **Bill Sharman**. "Ray, keep your elbow, wrist and shoulder in a straight line and the ball tends to go straight. Follow through with your wrist 'hanging over the rim.'" I was learning from the best.

I may have picked up some productive basketball skills from peers, but at that juncture, Sharman and Russell were of the best.

May we apply that principle to anger resolution. Learn from the best. What is the best source? Anger management skills are important; however, as Mitchell Messer, head of the anger clinic in

Chicago says, "**Anger management in the US doesn't get to the bottom line.**"

Dan Allender emphasizes this: "A bad temper may eventually be controlled by rage-reduction techniques. An angry person may come to mellow out over time. But the true **depths of destructive anger are only shaken to the core by the surprising grasp of the goodness of God. The Son took the cup of God's fury and drank it to its dregs so that even in our petty, self-righteous, demanding anger we would never taste a single drop of the Father's fury.**"

In the Bible, Joshua 1:8 tells us that if we meditate on Scripture and do what it says, we'll be successful. The Bible has no specific seven steps to successful anger resolution. But, I believe it has foundational principles that if understood and applied, brings us success in handling anger. It addresses the "bottom line."

Come with me in the next chapter to observe how many people are being set free from the destructiveness of unhealthy anger. Their anger quotient is dissipating. They feel better. Relationships are more meaningful.

Scripture:

Ephesians 4:31-32. *Get rid of all bitterness, rage and anger, brawling and slander, along with every form of malice. Be kind and compassionate to one another, forgiving each other, just as in Christ God forgave you.*

Exercise:

Which of the anger management techniques have you used that you've found helpful?_____

_____

_____

_____

Which of the anger management techniques have you tried but were found unsuccessful? _____

_____

_____

Which of the techniques will you consider trying? _____

_____

_____

_____

Any taming of another's wild beast you need to consider? How will you begin?

_____

_____

_____

_____

Prayer:
Father, clarify to me the techniques I can use to begin to tame the wild beast of mine and others.

Eleven
Let The Wild Beast Speak
Anger Resolution

Speak when angry and you'll make the best speech you'll ever regret. Bierce

We've addressed how **anger can be a gift** as we recognize what kind it is, process it appropriately and learn about ourselves from it. We've seen how **anger can be managed** in more productive ways then stuffing or venting.

Now, may I be so bold to say that **there is "remedy" for unhealthy anger**. Not a quick cure-all that sees an angry spirit dissipate over night; but, what I think is God's way of confronting unhealthy anger. A means to lessen the intensity and frequency that goes beyond anger management.

Because the Bible professes to be the guide to successful living, we must examine what it says about anger.

> More than anger management

The Bible on Anger
√ It is better to be *slow-tempered* than famous (Proverbs 16:32, TLB)
√ *Don't be quick-tempered - that is being a fool* (Ecclesiastes 7:9 TLB).
√ *It is best to listen much, speak little, and not become angry; for anger doesn't make us good as God demands that we must be* (James 1:19-20 TLB).
√ *Now is the time to cast off and throw away all these rotten garments of anger, hatred, cursing and dirty language* (Colossians 3:8 TLB).

1. Awareness

We've mentioned previously that it is not natural for a large segment of society to realize and face their anger. They are unaware of it. I wonder if the psalmist was concerned about his anger.

> *Search me, O God, and know my heart; test me and know my anxious thoughts. See if there is any offensive way in me, and lead me in the way everlasting.* Psalms 139:23-24

David also mentions <u>awareness</u> in Psalms19: 12-13

> *Who can discern his errors? Forgive my **hidden faults**. Keep your servant also from willful sins; may they not rule over me. Then will I be blameless, innocent of great transgression*

Covering attitudinal sins comes naturally. Most of us don't like to admit that we could be angry. Sometimes it is very hard to pray the **psalmist's "awareness prayer."** But

Show it to me, God

God often reveals it to us through dreams, reading of Scripture, prayer, confrontation with another person, and in our reactions to people.

Even then it is still difficult to say, **"Yes, I own my anger."** We would rather rationalize or defend ourselves. "If my wife just wouldn't cram the toothpaste tube, I wouldn't get angry," we say, still blaming the cause of our anger on someone else.

R.D.Palmer surveyed more than 500 hospitalized psychiatric and non-psychiatric patients. He found that the feature most characteristic of the group was **conflict involving fear** and inhibition, a **holding in, of angry feelings.**

> **These were people who wanted to lash out at others but felt guilty or anxious about their anger.**

Dr. Palmer saw these people not so much as being constantly filled with boiling anger; rather, they were **people easily provoked to anger.** When stirred up, they became anxious and tense with internal conflict, but still often denying the anger within them.

The first step to slaying the wild beast is to be aware of and accept how angry we really are.

2. Express

Once we allow God to bring to the surface our angry spirits, expression must take place. Mentioning again some of the anger management techniques: beat a pillow, scream. Some would say, "Imagine the person with whom you are angry sitting at a banquet, nude, eating

| Anger must be expressed |

with his fingers." Others suggest telephoning the person with whom he is angry and chewing him out, but keeping the finger on the cradle of the phone. Others suggest writing a letter expressing all the hate but not mailing it.

The Arabs have discovered **the camel has a great ability for hatred.** If the camel thinks the driver has mistreated it, it will bide its time before hurting the driver, but sooner or later it will retaliate. Anticipating this, the driver places his clothes in a conspicuous place, in the form of a sleeping man. When the camel sees the clothes, it tramples them viciously. The driver is then free of fear. The camel's rage has been vented.

How often do we also, in a fit of blind rage, have difficulty distinguishing between the real and the unreal - the fact and the prejudice?

Anger, even when justified, can quickly become exaggerated, irrational and overly dramatic.

(National Mental Health Assn.)

Among medical and psychological clinicians, there is a wide variation of philosophy regarding anger ventilation.

| Anger expression theories differ. |

Scream therapy was a prevalent mode of the past. Therapists would place people on the floor and teach them how to kick, beat, and scream, triggering past

125

memories. As they relived those memories, they'd scream out, freeing themselves from blockage. Big bucks were spent for this type of treatment.

A California psychologist was sued for a technique he called **rage reduction**. His theory was described by the claimant:

> **"I was tortured, including choking, beating, which included holding and tying me down and sticking fingers in my mouth."**

I suspect the person demonstrated great held-in rage and the therapist felt he had to trigger its expression. But it was a damaging and unethical counseling technique and provided for an expensive law suit.

Some ventilationists encourage **indiscriminate expression of anger in the counseling office**, like sticking pins into dolls, believing anger will be kept in proper bounds if dealt with clinically. But violence has a way of getting out of hand and can breed further violence. **Some people need stronger restraints to their anger.** Their quick tempers have spread devastation.

| Restrain anger or express it? | Most counseling professionals believe that ventilative therapies (get your anger out) can have positive results in treating anger-producing conflicts. |

As a person is encouraged to vent his feelings, his anxiety is reduced. The person learns that he isn't going to be punished for showing his resentment. He can admit to himself that anger does reside within him and not be bothered by the awareness.

However, Leonard Berkowtitz, who wrote some time ago in Psychology Today, stated:

> "The evidence dictates now that it is unintelligent to encourage persons to be aggressive even if, with the best of intentions, we want to limit such behavior to the confines of psychotherapy."

Dr. Milton Laden, as a member of the Psychiatric Department

of Johns Hopkins Medical School, supported the non expression of anger theory with,

> "Don't express anger. It is contagious,
> and as you express it, it returns back to you."

And, some studies do indicate that **the more we express rage, the more rageful we become.**

So, **how do we resolve these conflicting views of anger expression?** May we turn to the Bible and make an observation? King David was called a man after God's own heart. He certainly had his faults and sin, but his expression of anger in Psalm 109:6-15 might be a good pattern for us to follow.

> *Appoint an evil man to oppose him; let an accuser stand at his right hand. When he is tried, let him be found guilty, and may his prayers condemn him. May his days be few; may another take his place of leadership.* **May his children be fatherless and his wife a widow.** *May his children be wandering beggars; may they be driven from their ruined homes. May a creditor seize all he has; may strangers plunder the fruits of his labor. May no one extend kindness to him or take pity on his fatherless children.* **May his descendants be cut off,** *their names blotted out from the next generation. May the iniquity of his fathers be remembered before the LORD; may the sin of his mother never be blotted out. May their sins always remain before the LORD, that he may cut off the memory of them from the earth.*

David's expression of "turning it over to the Lord" reminds me of the challenge we have in 1 John 1:9 "If we confess..."

> I believe **anger, if not expressed, stays within us, contaminating us.**

Confession: the best form of expression

127

The best form of expression is some form of confession, like David's in Psalm 109. Ours may sound like: "God I'm really ticked off. My friend just hammered the emotional snot out of me. However, I realize I must be responsible for my reactions. He can't

> An irritant doesn't cause my anger. It reveals my angry spirit already there

make me angry. He is just revealing an angry spirit within me. God, forgive me. I believe you are not as interested in my venting this anger, as you are in freeing me from it. Do it, Father."

"But," you say, "what if I've just found that **my spouse is having an affair?** You expect me to confess my anger when it is my partner who is in bed with another person? You're crazy. They are the ones who need to be confessing."

True! That is what **they** should do. Their adulterous relationship is not only very destructive to all concerned, but is sin. BUT, **if we hang onto an angry response**, causing ourselves depression, anxiety and other physical complaints, we are being self-destructive (and sinful). **We are responsible for our reactions.** *If we confess...He is faithful...to forgive and cleanse...*

> "God, my spouse is being unfaithful. It is wrong. It hurts. I'm feeling like a zero. I've been hung. I'm angry. But God, take my angry spirit."

If our reaction of anger isn't resolved, it, along with the pain of abandonment, will destroy us.

At times, prayer must become even more elementary.

> "God, I am so angry, I don't even want to fool with resolving it. I'd rather get even or withdraw in silence. I know I need to Biblically process this for my own sake. Empower me to accept responsibility for my angry reaction."

Some would call that kind of prayer a cop-out. "God won't do for you what you can do for yourself," they insist. However, we can be hurt so deeply that all the human strength we can muster to activate our wills is not enough. There are times we need to apply Paul's promise:

God is at work within you, **helping you want to obey** *him, and then helping you do what he wants.* (Philippians 2:13 TLB).

Have you ever felt the person with whom you were angry deserved at least a day of your silent treatment, or at least ten minutes of chewing out. It's not that you want them to hurt so deeply. You want them to feel the pain they caused you. You want to get even a bit.

Suggested prayer: "God, help me be willing to let this go."

A friend of mine gets periodic shock treatments because he is unwilling to let go of anger. Irritations build and continue to fester, until, as his psychiatrist says, "**We need to scramble your brains to help you forget the situations that have made you so angry.**" Obviously, the ECT is not solving the problem.

3. Express to the source?

Do we just express anger in prayer? Should we express our feelings to the person who has triggered the anger within us?

The Bible says,

A wise man restrains his anger (Proverbs 19:11, TLB).

In other words, don't blow up!

Get over your anger quickly,

Paul exhorts us in Ephesians 4:26.

"Hey, that sounds like I must be a doormat and let people walk all over me," someone may say. "If I restrain my anger and get over it quickly, he will get away with 'murder.'"

Anger is going to come out somehow; especially, and particularly in marriage. Though our partner is not venting anger, we can sense it. Actions speak. "Vibrations" send messages. Flying vases indicate something is amiss.

One of our dear friends, who is now with the Lord, described her honeymoon anger.

"Nelson did something that really irritated me. Before I knew it, I had one of our beautiful wedding gifts, a **valuable vase** in my hand, my arm cocked, ready to fire it at him. I thought of the results: a shattered vase. So **I rolled it at him**! We both nearly 'died' laughing."

> Honeymoon
> Anger
> Expression

An open relationship, marital or not, involves communication. Especially in marriage, situations causing anger need to be communicated, but not in an attacking way. Not, "You stinkin' louse! What did you do that for? I hate your guts! I wish I hadn't married you."

A. The **first step** in interpersonal expression is **WAIT!** Psalms 37: 7-8 tells us:

WAIT

> *Be still before the LORD and wait patiently for him; do not fret when men succeed in their ways, when they carry out their wicked schemes. Refrain from anger and turn from wrath; do not fret—it leads only to evil.*

We wait as a first step because **initial anger is usually very rash and usually damaging**. Harm is averted to self or the other, if we wait.

Waiting also gives us **time to clarify underlying issues** surrounding our anger. It allows me to ask tough questions about myself. The Psalmist tells us to wait in 4:4:

> *In your anger do not sin; when you are on your beds, search your hearts and be silent.*

"This person can't make me mad. He/she is only bringing out what is inside of me. Is my anger holy? Healthy? Unholy? If unholy, is it a sign of selfishness, self-protectiveness? Is a buried wound being pricked? How am I being exposed? God, give me 20-20 vision into myself."

Insight is processed with The Father. Healing, appropriated where necessary. Grace, claimed for self and the other. **Learning and growth takes place**.

B. <u>Step two</u>. After waiting, **communication begins**. "What you did really triggered my anger." State what your desires are to rectify the situation. Both parties express their view. Sometimes an agreement can be negotiated. The problem is either worked out or agreement to disagree takes place.

Henri Nouwen suggests:

> "Do not hesitate to talk about angry feelings even when they are related to very small or seemingly insignificant issues. **When you don't deal with anger on small issues, how will you ever be ready to deal with it in a real crisis?** Your anger can have good reasons. Talk to me about it. Maybe I made the wrong decision, maybe I have to change my mind. If I feel that your anger is unrealistic or disproportionate, then we can have a closer look at what made you respond too strongly."

At times, the **other party is too insecure, too easily threatened** to handle an expression of anger. Or we may be trying to **break a pattern of always spewing anger**. Consequently, anger is directed vertically instead of horizontally. "God, I'm angry" and the details are enumerated.

As the anger is confronted with God, then it is less threatening for the other person to receive the conflict communication. They are more readily able to hear something like, "You know, I've just conquered a bit of my anger. But I know that you want us to have a growing marriage relationship and for communication's sake I want you to know that it really hurt when you — forgot my birthday today."

Notice the dynamics here.
- **The person has faced, expressed and resolved the anger within.**
- No buildup of destructive physical, psychological, or spiritual symptoms.
- Communication continued with the partner, building an open and growing relationship.
- No doormat here.
- No venting out of control here.

The "wild beast," being tamed, has spoken in respectful, expressive, constructive communication

But there is more. Anger is not resolved yet. Let's slay the beast. Next chapter.

———————————

Scripture:
> Psalm 4:4 *In your anger do not sin; when you are on your beds, search your hearts and be silent.*
> Ephesians 4:26-27 *In your anger do not sin: Do not let the sun go down while you are still angry, and do not give the devil a foothold.*

Exercise:

All of us get angry at times. It could be a slight irritation or it might be an outright hate. How are you doing communicating that anger? To God. _____

To people. _____

Can you think of an angering situation, past or present, that needs to be discussed with the other person? _____

_____

Think through and write your strategy. _____

_____

_____

Can you project what will be the other person's response?

_____

_____

How will you handle that response? _____

_____

_____

Prayer:

Father, it is my desire to be conflict-free with everyone, if possible. Help me think through my issues and be responsible for my attitude. Empower me to go to the other person and speak the truth in love with a goal of reconciliation between and freedom within.

Twelve
Slay the Wild Beast
Anger Source Resolved

*If a small thing has the power to make you angry,
does that not indicate something about your size?* Harris

A little old man repeatedly stood up in church during testimony time and with a breaking voice of confession would always say, referring to the sins in his life, "I am such an evil man. I hate. I lust. I worry. I doubt God. Lord, clean out the cobwebs of my heart." Every Sunday night, during that part of the service, he would follow the same pattern. "Lord, clean out the cobwebs of my heart."

A little old lady grew weary of his weekly lament, couldn't stand it any longer and after his last confession, piped up, "Lord, don't just clean out the cobweb, **kill the spider**."

The man was dealing with his sin. She was suggesting dealing with the source—the sinner.

Is anger sin? Is awareness and expression through confession a sufficient remedy for slaying the wild beast?

Some thoughts. **Unhealthy anger that is so destructive,** that it hurts our bodies, spirits and relationships, **can easily be labeled as sin**. But I'm more concerned about the underlying **cause of <u>most</u> of our unhealthy anger and that is selfishness**. "I'm not getting my way at my time." Or, "You're intruding on my turf." To me that is a greater "sin," a greater destructiveness. It is also the source of most of our anger!

Is Anger Sin?

"Hey, Burwick," you may be saying, "**Christ got angry and He didn't sin.** Besides, if you lived with what I have to live with, you would be angry, too. And, by the way, Paul wrote that we should '**be angry and sin not**'" (Ephesians 4:26).

Christ was angry. Paul encouraged anger - ?

Some interpret this scripture as a command to be angry. But this does not seem to fit the context because five verses later Paul wrote: "Let all bitterness, and wrath, and anger ... be put away from you" (verse 31).

The belief I hold is this: **in the original writing of scripture there were no punctuation marks. This could be a question: be (are) you angry? If so, don't hang on to it. Don't let it spend the night. Even if it is holy anger (unselfish anger which is not sin), such anger can become sin if one lets it linger without constructively resolving it.**

Christ's anger? Examine the root. It was **not the result of selfishness**. In contrast, as we examine the root of most of our anger, we see that it is usually motivated by selfishness. An attitude of "I'm not getting my way," or, "You're invading my turf."

We looked at the need for expression of anger in the last chapter. Expression through confession brings a release and is productive, but **if the focus is the anger and not the cause, anger will not permanently dissipate.** It will continue its contaminating pattern. So we must dig deeper.'

DEATH TO SELF—ALIVE IN CHRIST

Confess sin. Die to self. Let C.S. Lewis describe it in Joyful Christian:

"The **self can be regarded in two ways.** On the one hand, it is **God's creature**, an occasion of love and rejoicing... On the other hand, it is that one self of others which is called I and me, and which on that ground puts forward an **irrational claim to preference**. This claim is to be not only hated, but simply killed; 'never,' as George MacDonald says, 'to be allowed a moment's respite from eternal death.' The Christian must wage endless war against the ego..."

The "good self," created in God's image. The "bad self," called "flesh," turning to its own way.

> **The root cause of most anger is "the flesh,"**
> **the <u>self</u> gone awry (the irrational claim to preference.)**

- The <u>self</u> is the individual's unique gift from God, the **basis of individuality**.
- <u>Self</u> **is the bearer of the divine image** (created in the image of God).
- However, <u>self</u> gone awry, turned into itself (flesh), becomes the source for temptation, then sin.
- The <u>self</u>, when focusing on self-protection or self-gratification, easily succumbs to "if I don't get my way; or, if I feel threatened, I get angry."

If a perceived need is not met, we get angry. If our position is threatened, we get angry. In summary, **if we have an expectation and it isn't met, the result is anger.** The "I" (the flesh) must die. What does that mean?

The concept of "death to self" and "resurrected with Christ" is the most dynamic concept I have witnessed in the field of biblical counseling. Charles

> *The "I" must die*

Solomon with his <u>Handbook to Happiness</u> spearheaded this movement. Bill Gilham and <u>Lifetime Guarantee</u> added to the resources, coupled with a host of others who have written about the "exchanged life," "deeper life," "the cross life" and similar topics.

Paul wrote in Galatians 2:20,

> *I am crucified with Christ; nevertheless,*
> *I live; yet not I, but **Christ lives in me.***

Paul explained in another place,

> *Knowing this, that our **old man is crucified** with him (Christ),*
> *that the body of sin might be destroyed,*
> *that henceforth we should not serve sin (Romans 6:6).*

May we insert "selfish anger" in place of "sin"? "...that the body of (selfish anger) might be destroyed, that henceforth we should not serve (selfish anger.)"

The sin nature, the old man within us, the unbelieving, unre-

| "Flesh" contrasted with the "old nature" |

pentant person before accepting Christ, died with Christ when we received him as Savior and Lord; consequently, we need not be controlled by that old nature any longer. Its power has been shattered. Elaboration can be found in Romans chapters six through eight, Philippians three and in Colossians chapters one through three.

The old nature died, 2 Corinthians 5:17 tells us:

Therefore, if anyone is in Christ, he is a new creation;
the old has gone, the new has come!

However, there still is a self, call it "flesh," that can respond to temptation and think and behave ungodly. This is the dimension within us that fears, worries, lusts, wants its own way, etc. Romans 8:13 tells us to habitually put to death (deaden) the flesh. The old nature (the before Christ person) is dead. However, there is still a flesh (self) that must be reckoned with continually.

Out of this "death concept" comes an awareness of our true life in Christ.

This book is not meant to explore deeply the concepts referred to as "identification with Christ." No point in attempting to duplicate excellent material (like Solomon's and Gilham's) already available which focuses on this distinctive quality of life. However, let's take a cursory look at who Christians really are in Christ.

MY TRUE IDENTITY

Understanding how Christ's death was the sacrifice needed for our sins (**justification**) is easily accepted by most Christians. As we see how Christ's blood was shed for us, we can appropriate his forgiveness and are cleansed from sins.

Too many of us stop with this insight and are left, as it were, in a **spiritual squirrel cage** - sinning and confessing, sinning and confessing. Anger explodes or implodes. We confess it. But a short time later the snares of selfish anger thoroughly entrap us again. We confess again. "Is there any freedom from the angry spirit that seems to consume us?" we wonder.

This position of need is beneficial to the Christian. **Without recognition of need there is no desire for growth.**

We are not only to see Christ's **death for our sins**. We must also become aware of the liberating

| Contrast "sin" |
| with |
| "Sin nature" |

truth of being crucified with Christ **to our sin nature**. Christ, hanging on the cross, bleeding and dying, paid the penalty for our unhealthy anger. The blood cleanses.

But, Christ also **took us to the cross with him** that we may be delivered from our selfish nature that underlies most of our anger. The Holy Spirit wants to bring us to freedom from the power of our selfish/angry nature.

And if the Spirit of him who raised Jesus from the dead is living in you, he who raised Christ from the dead will also give life to your mortal bodies through his Spirit, who lives in you. Romans 8:11. The Holy Spirit is our "powerhouse" for freedom.

Paul elaborates in 2 Corinthians 5:14, 17, 21,
> *Since we believe that Christ died for all of us, we should also believe that* **we have died to the old life we used to live** *.... When someone becomes a Christian he becomes a brand new person inside. He is not the same any more. A new life has begun....For God took the sinless Christ and poured into him our sins. Then in exchange,* **he poured God's goodness into us!**

"Christus Victor" – Christ conquered Satan, sin and death. Through our co-crucifixion with Him we have died to our self-centered natures. We are completely **freed from sins' <u>power</u>** whether we take advantage of the freedom or not.

"Hold it, Burwick," you may be thinking. "Are you preaching eradication - sinless perfection? I know I am crucified with Christ, but the best I can do with my angry nature is try to control it. Do you mean I can actually be freed from it?"

Yes, <u>becoming</u> **free from the control of sin** is the flawless provision of God's grace. **It is not that we cannot sin; but, that we can live without sin.**

> *My little children, I am telling you that*
> *so that you will stay away from sin* (1 John 2:1, TLB).

This accomplished fact becomes reality in our experience as moment by moment we count it to be fact. Romans 6:11 tells us:

> *In the same way, count yourselves dead to sin but alive to God in Christ Jesus.*

Paul continues with elaboration in the following three verses:

> *Therefore* **do not let sin reign in your mortal body** *so that you obey its evil desires.* **Do not offer the parts of your body to sin,** *as instruments of wickedness, but rather offer yourselves to God, as those who have been brought from death to life; and offer the parts of your body to him as instruments of righteousness. For* **sin shall not be your master,** *because you are not under law, but under grace.*

We may have felt imprisoned in the dingiest, darkest, slimiest, **hellhole cell of anger's prison,** and have long since given up making scratch marks on the wall to record the passing of days and years in prison.

| A smiling mask over a body of anger. |

A way of escape consumes our minds. We've **expressed** our anger, which has seemed to cause only more. We've **stuffed** our anger and our bodies and minds have suffered greatly. We've tried to **discuss rationally** our anger in the throes of conflict, but it always seemed to boil out of control We've **gone to the altar** at church; we've **confessed** over and over; and we've worn our plastic smiling Christian faces. But anger is still with us.

Until...

Dialogue With Christ

The cell door opens. **There stands the Master.**

"What are you doing in here?" He asks. "Don't you know who you are? Do you want to be released from this prison? *You shall know the truth and the truth shall set you free.*"

"Yes, Master, what is the truth? I want to be free from this all-consuming propensity to anger."

Therefore, brothers, we have an obligation—but it is not to the sinful nature, to live according to it. For if you live according to the sinful nature, you will die; but if __by the Spirit you put to death the misdeeds of the body__ (the flesh), you will live, because those who are led by the Spirit of God are sons of God. Romans 8:12-14

Christ continues speaking, "You (your sin-loving nature) died with me on the cross when I died. You are no longer under sin's power to think and act in a self-centered way. The flesh that gets so angry when it is threatened or doesn't get its way must be crushed. Count on that as **fact** and **action**, moment by moment.

"Yield your whole life to me. Yield those rights and expectations, those desires that push your anger button if they are not fulfilled. I have much more available to you than what your puny flesh desires. As you follow this 'yielded totally to Me' pattern, The Holy Spirit will make freedom real to you. Through conflicts the truth will become established in you as you yield to the Holy Spirit's power.

"Be patient. Lifestyles don't change over night. As you see your position in Me through studying the Word and yielding to it, the Holy Spirit slowly and gently changes your lifestyle. Anger-producing situa-

Becoming free

tions are more quickly conquered. You'll find yourself becoming slower to anger.

"Let's move on out of this prison cell. You are (becoming) free."

It is most important that we **saturate our minds with Scripture** - like Romans chapters 6 through 8 and allow the Holy Spirit to deeply teach us our identity in Christ. Ian Thomas, Miles Stanford, Ruth Paxton, and many other authors have excellent material which develops more fully the identification-with-Christ dynamic described here.

As each day finds us on our knees with Scripture in hand, "renewing our minds" (reminding ourselves that we are not only God's children, but are actually filled through and through with the Creator), our minds are set on our true identity. As we face challenges of the day that could produce anger, **we can quickly remind ourselves of who we really are and lessen the tendency to drink the poisons of self-centered anger**.

For instance, we have the natural expectation of someone close

Expectation leads to demand, which leads to anger

to us meeting a specific need of ours. "I've worked especially hard for this person. I deserve a compliment." The compliment does not come. Our expectation is not met. The natural temptation is to be hurt and angry.

Ideally, as soon as the temptation presents itself, we may remind ourselves that we don't have to yield to it. The psalmist wrote,

> *My soul, wait only upon God;*
> *for my expectation is from him* (Psalms 62:5).

We **can desire** but **not expect** from anyone, except God, who has promised to supply all our needs (Philippians 4:19). If we really believe these verses and put them into practice, selfish anger and its devastation diminishes.

However, the ideal is not always achieved. We often hold onto expectations. They often become demands. Anger grows.

When we find ourselves in the throes of anger, we can quickly say:

> "Hold it. I am not thinking and acting like who I really am. My old nature died with Christ. I'm a new creation in Him. He wants to meet all my needs. I don't have to be controlled by the flesh. I choose to crush my demanding flesh (die to self). I am alive with the Creator of the universe, who is permeating my very being. He is my strength. He is my life. He is my forgiveness for the unforgivable. He is my love for the unlovely."

Thus we are putting into **action** the INSIGHT we gathered through our study and through the teaching and empowerment of the Holy Spirit.

Jesus said, *Deny (yourself) and take up (your) cross daily* (Luke 9:23). Crush the deeds and the thinking of that self-centered self - daily!

Importance of balance: insight followed by action

Paul wrote in Romans 6:11,

Reckon yourselves to be dead indeed unto sin. In other words, remind yourself of the challenge is to daily squash the deeds and thoughts of our self-centered self.

This is the application. The **action**. The putting into practice or the "shoe leather" of what we know to be true about ourselves (**insight**). If we leave out either insight or action, there will be dysfunction.

Insight-oriented people have a tendency to sit back and **expect God to do everything.** **Action-oriented people** take to heart that "pseudo scripture" which says "God helps those who help themselves." Their focus is, "You have to die to self," and they tend to lie on their bed of spikes or crawl a mile on their stomachs, killing self - self annihilation.

143

The Bible does say, "Mortify (kill) *the deeds of the body* (Romans 8:13). This is important, but it is a lot easier to "die to self" when our minds have been saturated with the concept that the power of our sinful nature is shattered. We don't have to be controlled by it. We just need to act on it, and yield to who we really are.

Out of our **identification with Christ in death** comes our **identification with Christs in resurrection.**

Behavior
Self Talk

Paraphrasing Paul's words: *It is not I who lives, but Christ through me!* Christ is our SOURCE for life.

Consider how this principle might be worked out in an actual life situation:

"God, I'm angry at my husband. What he did to me was wrong, and **he is responsible for his behavior.** But **I am responsible for my reaction** of anger. I confess it. Take it, God. **Change ME.** I die to the right of having a loving husband who will put me first. I yield to **my position of resurrection with Christ.** Lord, you are my security when my husband is not. You are my love when he refuses to love me. You are my strength. By the power of your Holy Spirit forgive my husband through me. Love him through me." **THAT IS INSIGHT.**

Then she should look for ways to allow God to express that loving, forgiving spirit through her to her husband. And love might have two components in this situation. Tender love bakes him his favorite pie. "Tough love" gently confronts him with his selfishness! **THAT IS ACTION.**

Personalizing this: many years ago, my first wife and I were near divorce. Our marriage was a hellish mess. We were both working through some scars in our backgrounds, and we were really spewing a lot of emotional garbage on each other. Through this trauma, plus **severe pregnancy problems** for Ann, and then the **death of one of our twin boys**, we were brought to the end of ourselves - a state of desperation.

> **Our marriage was a hellish mess.**

I am convinced that God allows such circumstances as this to happen so that we can **see the utter futility of living in the power of "self."** He brings us to the experience Paul spoke of in Romans 7:18: *...in me (that is in my flesh) dwells no good thing.*

Only then are we ready for living by the power of the Holy Spirit as described in Romans chapter 8. Only then do we relate to Paul's words:

> *...not because we think we can do anything of lasting value by ourselves. Our only power and success comes from God* (2 Corinthians 3:5 TLB)

As this concept became the focus for Ann and me (instead of pointing a finger at each other), **God began to do drastic work within us**. We individually began to pray, "Jesus, the power of my sinful self is broken. I don't have to be controlled by bitterness. I reckon (count on) my flesh-life to be dead."

As we prayed like that, our appropriate desires that had evolved into selfish expectations which became demands, were crushed. **Bitterness slowly dissipated.**

But there was **still a void**. Positional death with Christ was becoming an experiential reality. Bitterness was gone. The only **feeling** was emptiness.

Love feelings return

Resurrection with Christ (experientially) had not come into play. I remember very distinctly praying for 30 days straight, "God, I can't love Ann the way you command me to love her. I want to. You **love her through me!**" (We had both hurt each other deeply, destroying our love feelings.)

I looked for ways to allow God to express his love through me, even buying her a rose, although I did not feel like it. On the thirtieth day of the "action love" and

> Love feelings return

the prayer commitment, I noticed a little spark, as the feeling of love began to return. Our love for each other did return and continued to deepen until her sudden death after 36 years of marriage.

The mechanics of this concept, called **"identification with**

Christ" are much easier to put into shoe leather (action) as greater insights are gained.

An interesting slant to this concept is provided by W.T. Purkiser:

> "We have a sinful self to be crucified by Christ,
> a human self to be controlled by Christ,
> in order that the true self may be realized in Christ."

Some of my clients, while studying identification Scriptures and related material have a **very emotional experience**. "Wow! I see! My old self-life died with Christ, and he now lives in and through me." Burdens are lifted, bondage is broken and the heavens open.

For some, **growth comes through little glimpses of the truth** spread over months and years. Our loving heavenly Father gives to his children what we need at the right time, and only as we need it!

In summary: we **don't just "manage"** anger. We **don't just release** anger. Roots of unhealthy anger must be confronted. The core is the "flesh," the individual's unique gift from God that has gone awry, turned inward, focusing on self-protection or self-gratification.

The course that is often taken looks like this: legitimate desires often evolve into fleshly expectations. Expectations lead to demands, which, not met, lead to anger.

Flesh must be squashed. The selfish, demanding self, the root of most of our anger, must die daily. Focus then is redirected from self to life in Christ. He desires to be the source for our expectations. He wants to meet our needs, to fulfill our desires.

Anger resolution: Death to self. Life in Christ.

Come with me to the last chapter in the book, focusing on personal growth.

Scripture:

146

Galatians 2:20 *I have been crucified with Christ and I no longer live, but Christ lives in me. The life I live in the body, I live by faith in the Son of God, who loved me and gave himself for me.*

Prayer:

Father, show me where my **desires** have evolved into **selfish expectations** and demands. Show me more deeply how I am not thinking and acting like who I really am in You. Empower me to crush the deeds of my demanding, self-centered flesh and look to how I can allow You to live Your life through me.

Exercise:

Where in my life am I not getting my way and need to "die to self" so that Christ can meet my need? _____

_____

To whom in my life do I need to give Christ's love - tenderly?

_____

To whom in my life do I need to give Christ's tough love?

_____

I commit to reading Romans 6-8 daily for a month. yes ___ no ___

Suggested reading:

Handbook to Happiness, Charles Solomon
Lifetime Guarantee, Bill Gilham
The Calvary Road, Roy Hession
Principles of Spiritual Growth, Miles Stanford
The Saving Life of Christ, Ian Thomas
The Normal Christian Life, Watchman Nee
Destined for the Throne, Paul Billheimer
Destined for the Cross, Paul Billheimer
Search for Significance, Robert McGee

Thirteen
Take Two Tablets

Personal Growth - Unhealthy Anger Prevention

...becoming conformed to the image of Christ. Romans 8:29

A tongue in cheek story of the Old Testament is told about Moses and God having a dialogue. Moses: "God, these children of Israel are a stubborn stiff-necked, murmuring, rebellious people. They give me a headache."

God: "Moses, here, take two tablets..."

It'd be nice if two tablets (pills) could correct our self-centered worries, fears, lust, anger, etc. The "tablets" for you and me really represent a **strategic plan for our growth**, our emotional and spiritual maturation. As we grow in our journey with God, not only seeing him as a God of justice but also observing His loving care and grace to us, we have less need to fear, to worry, to covet, to be selfishly angry.

We find man's basic challenge in Jeremiah 9:23-24:

*This is what the LORD says: "Let not the wise man boast of his wisdom or the strong man boast of his strength or the rich man boast of his riches, but let him who boasts boast about this: **that he understands and knows me**, that I am the LORD, who exercises **kindness, justice and righteousness** on earth, for in these I delight," declares the LORD.*

As we know God more intimately, we realize at deeper levels that He is, as Romans 8 describes Him, our loving Abba PaPa, (Heavenly Daddy), working everything out for our good as we endeavor to walk close to Him.

Do you have a **strategic plan for growth in godliness** - one that roots out the core of unhealthy anger?

PERSONAL GROWTH TRIAD

This growth plan begins with **authenticity** - living honestly. Demasking. Frederick Buechner expresses this phenomenon in Telling Secrets:

> "Our original shimmering self gets buried so deep we hardly live out of it at all...rather, we learn to live out of all the other selves which we are constantly putting on and taking off like coats and hats against the world's weather."

We must define our "other selves," the masks we wear, repudiate them and realize that **transformation of our being begins with the <u>mind</u>.**

Our mind: the vehicle for growth

Paul tells us about this in Romans 12:2:

Do not conform any longer to the pattern of this world, but be transformed by the renewing of your mind.

"Transformed" is from the Greek "metamorphosis": from ugly crawling worm into a cocoon out of which evolves a beautiful butterfly. "Be metamorphosed (be butter-flied) by the renewing of the mind."

Dr. Frank Minirth, world renown Christian psychiatrist, gives us some insight into transformation as he writes in Christian Counseling Today, "**Simple behavioral Scriptural techniques are so powerful.** I think they have the ability to **change the brain's chemistry**. What we see comes into the eyes, into the frontal lobe. It will rearrange the neurotransmitters. The neurotransmitters rearrange secondary messenger systems that store memory. So **who we are to some degree is controlled by what we take in.**

> "Therefore, the more Scripture we take in, especially loving it and enjoying it, really changes the very essence of who we are."

Memorize more Scripture

Dr. Minirth goes on to say, "So the emphasis, I hope, in the future will be to get people to **memorize more Scripture** so it can change them. The more Christ-like we become, the more He can remove symptoms."

Symptoms like: anxiety, fear, unhealthy anger, depression, poor self esteem, etc. that are often caused by wrong mindsets. Mindsets not corresponding to the mind of Christ.

The popular psychologist Philip McGraw makes a strong "mindset" point in his book <u>Self Matters.</u> He puts an end to the common **"victim role"** that has taken hold of our culture.

| We are <u>not</u> victims! |

He suggests we address the
- ✓ ten most **defining moments** of life,
- ✓ the seven most **critical choices** and the
- ✓ five most **pivotal people** in our world and understand how they shaped us.

This "shaping" produced in us a mindset that often determines our lifestyle - how we see ourselves and how we live out that self perception, which usually has negative elements. **We don't need to be stuck in a mindset that is not productive and results in little personal growth.**

For the nuts and bolts, the fundamentals of personal growth, may I simplify it by using a triad graphic.

Work of the Holy Spirit

Biblical World View   Self-Discipline

At one of the bases of the growth triangle are the words **"Biblical world view:"**

The other base is **"Self discipline"**. The apex of the triad is **"Work of the Holy Spirit."**

Let's examine each while addressing the issue of personal growth.

Biblical world view

This represents the grid through which people interpret life's experiences. It is our response to life's events, (a human response and, as Christians, superhuman.)

Human response:

The Psalms expose **David's** human feelings. Chapter 109: "...kill my enemies. Make their widows to be childless...")

In Gethsemane, **Christ's** human emotions are revealed: Luke 22:44

> *And being in anguish, he prayed more earnestly, and his sweat was like drops of blood falling to the ground.*

Christ didn't spiritualize by saying "all things work for good...." He was not only fully divine but also fully human. He had real human feelings. **He was carrying the weight of the world's sin on his shoulders and the human part of him was dreading crucifixion.**

Likewise, we should not repress or spiritualize, but be human. It is natural to hurt, to fear, to resent. Some Christians in their desire to be godly don't allow themselves to sense human feelings - to be | Be human, then be superhuman |
angry, to fear, to worry, to hurt. Consequently, feelings become repressed and resurface through some form of emotional, physical or relational pain (as described in earlier chapters).

Your world view first reveals your humanity, your human thoughts and feelings. But we don't stop there. As believers in and followers of Jesus Christ, we can then react with:

<u>Superhuman response</u>

James 1:2-4: *Consider it pure joy, my brothers, whenever you face trials of many kinds, because you know that the testing of your faith develops perseverance. Perseverance must finish its work so that you may be mature and complete, not lacking anything.*

And Romans 5:3-5 emphasizes this concept ... *we also rejoice (exult, boast) in our sufferings, because we know that suffering produces perseverance; perseverance, character; and character, hope....*

Tough times are not pleasant.

The process is painful.

But the product is of great value.

Character, not lacking anything, is formed.

I haven't enjoyed the last three years of **Parkinson's Disease**. It is embarrassing. I walk funny. Eating is difficult. Memory is dissipating. I'm very slow moving. I shake. Balance is a challenge. I "freeze," where my body won't move. And other inconveniences. I would prefer not having Parkinson's. My wife and I have prayed for healing. People with the gift of healing have prayed for me, all to no avail.

I relate well with Paul in 2 Corinthians 12:8:

Three times I pleaded with the Lord to take it

(the thorn in his flesh) *away from me.*

But it seemed as if God said to me like He did to Paul in verse 9:

My grace is sufficient for you, for my

power is made perfect in weakness.

The process of Parkinson's has been painful but the product has been:

- A deepening **dependency on the God for even little tasks**.
- An ever intensifying awareness of my **need for intimacy with "Abba Papa."**
- Influencing others to trust God.

> The process, painful, yet the product of great value.

- Shaking sometimes signals an inner stress – a feeling of inadequacy, a self focus that needs rectifying.
- A humbling agent.
- Purging the idolatry of performance for approval and recognition.
- A testing of my faith, hope and endurance. And a lot of **character growth** that if I enumerate, I'll get cocky and ruin the whole process.

It'd be easy to have a **human** attitude of **resentment** with a **bit of self-pity** thrown in. When the **superhuman** takes over, I began to see Parkinson's from God's eyes. I began to see it as the character building challenge that it is, and Parkinson's becomes more acceptable. **A Biblical world view.**

Christ sets the **ultimate example of a Biblical world view.** Through his human emotions in Gethsemane he comes to a place of relinquishment. Luke 22:42:

Father, if you are willing, take this cup from me;
yet not my will, but yours be done.

As we mature in our walk with God, we take on a more realistic Biblical world view that might say:

"I don't like what I'm experiencing, 'yet not my will but yours' because I know by faith that you, Father, are using this for my good and your glory."

With Christ developing His attitude in me, I can now say I wouldn't exchange the years of Parkinson's for freedom even if I could. I would prefer freedom from Parkinson's! I would like to have the product without the pain. **The process is painful, yet the product (growth in character) is of great value!**

John Wesley says it succinctly. *"How innumerable are the benefits which God conveys to the children of men through the channel of sufferings! — so that it might be said, 'What are termed afflictions in the language of men, are in the language of God styled blessings.'"*

Joseph is another **example of seeing life from a Biblical world view.** After being abused and abandoned by his brothers, he admonished them, Genesis 50:20:

> *You intended to harm me, but God intended it for good to accomplish what is now being done, the saving of many lives.*

As we take on the Joseph maturity, initial human reactions are more quickly processed with God and we know more clearly how He is working everything to our good and His glory. As we become more mature in Christ, we can handle anything that life can throw at us. An obvious result is less self-centeredness and fear; consequently, less anger.

Our **Biblical World View** is followed by the other side of the growth triad base labeled:

• Self discipline

It has been said that discipline is the <u>bridge</u> between goals and accomplishments.

2 Peter 1:5-10 speaks of discipline:

> *For this very reason, **make every effort** to add to your faith goodness; and to goodness, knowledge; and to knowledge, **self-control**; and to self-control, perseverance; and to perseverance, godliness; and to godliness, brotherly kindness; and to brotherly kindness, love ... For if you do these things, you will never fall.*

Do you catch the emphasis:

<u>self-control, make every effort, discipline, self-discipline, to add to your faith</u>?

155

| Is self-discipline legalism? |

"Whoa, Burwick, **sounds like legalism**. Taking scriptures out of context. A gospel of works. I've been that route. Got frustrated and burned out. Nearly gave up on God."

Hear me out. When I'm speaking of discipline in the Christian walk, I'm not saying that our acceptance with God depends on what we do. Ephesians 2:8-9 is clear that our acceptance from God commences and continues by faith. The whole book of Galatians places emphasis on Grace over works.

Discipline is not for salvation or acceptance from God, but
discipline is the part we play in the growth process.

King Solomon saw it so important that he states in the first chapter of Proverbs that the book was written to teach people wisdom and <u>discipline.</u>

The Bible uses **athletics as a metaphor for self discipline.**
I Corinthians. 9:24:

> *Do you not know that in a race all the runners run,*
> *but only one gets the prize?   Run in such a way as to*
> *get the prize.* (**Discipline of the runner.**)

Philippians 3:14:

> *I press on toward the goal to win the prize for which*
> *God has called me heavenward in Christ Jesus.*
> (**Discipline toward the goal.**)

Discipline, being a disciple of Jesus, will bear fruit:
John 15:8:

> *This is to my Father's glory, that you bear much fruit,*
> *showing yourselves to be my disciples.*

And the ultimate result:
2 Timothy 4:7-8:

> *I have fought the good fight, I have finished the race, I*
> *have kept the faith. Now there is in store for me the*
> *crown of righteousness, which the Lord, the righteous*
> *Judge, will award to me on that day—and not only to*
> *me, but also to all who have longed for his appearing.*

The ultimate result: **eternity with Jesus**.

In-depth reading on the disciplines of the Christian life can be found in Richard Foster's book <u>Celebration of Discipline</u> and Dallas Willard's <u>The Spirit of the Disciplines</u>.

A growth plan must be structured around disciplines of the spiritual life, not for salvation, not for God's approval, but for aggressive maturity in Christ.

Steps to self-discipline

For the person who lacks self discipline,

1. the first step in growth seems to be **observing the loss that comes through <u>lack</u> of self-discipline.** The lack of accomplishment from procrastination. The lack of desired spiritual growth. The pain of regret with which this loss is associated. **REPENT of the laziness - the lack of self discipline. Discipline pain is inevitable. <u>We either experience the pain of structuring a self-disciplined life or the pain of regret from lack of self discipline.</u>**

First, observe the loss and then repent (turn it around, go the other way).

2. Next, acknowledge the need for the **ninth fruit of the spirit - self control** which is interpreted "self-discipline." Pray something like, "Father, I have been haphazard in planning. I've been lazy in following through. I've not followed Christ into his own practices of discipline. Help me develop and stick to a plan of growth. As I extend effort, empower me with your Holy Spirit. I provide the vessel. You provide the power.

The discipline of <u>engagement</u>

Willard suggests that in the Christian life there are two basic disciplines: **the discipline of <u>engagement</u> and the discipline of <u>abstinence</u>.** We'll look first at engagement.

Scheduling the week in advance - what needs to be done and when, is a plan that many people find helpful. Following the plan rigidly for a few weeks begins to build a pattern of discipline. After this standard of discipline becomes more a part of life, rigidity can be backed off somewhat to a more flexible schedule. Sometimes an accountability partner to "report in to" is helpful in turning the self-discipline problem around.

Someone may ask, "What were **Christ's discipline practices?**"

- Solitude and silence.
- He was a student of Scripture.
- He engaged in worship, prayer and service.
- Exercise. He walked a lot!

Solitude liberates and prepares us for study. Andrew Bonar

| Significance of solitude |

writes: "in order to grow in grace, we must spend a great deal of time in quiet solitude. Contact with others in society is not what causes the soul to grow most vigorously. In fact, **one quiet hour of prayer will often yield greater results than many days spent in the company of others.**" (Streams in the Desert)

Our <u>discipline of engagement</u> **curriculum for Christ-likeness** might include;

- memorizing the 10 commandments, the Lord's Prayer, the Sermon on the Mount, Romans 8, Colossians 3, Philippians 2-4. <u>This can be an essential part of any curriculum for becoming like Christ.</u> Positive engagement with these scriptures will bring kingdom order into our entire personality. We significantly come to think and believe in a godly manner and that changes our every outlook for the good.
- Be unbending in your study of Jesus. Follow Him into His practices and adapt them to form an effective framework of spiritual disciplines around which your whole life can be structured.

- Worship must be a part of discipline to complete the renewal of our minds. Through worship we embrace the radiant Person of God who is worthy of all praise. **Study and memorizing Scripture without worship so easily leads to spiritual pride.**

In worship we are ascribing greatness, goodness and glory to God. It **imprints** on our whole being the **reality**, the **power** and the **value** in following Christ.

> Are you being imprinted?

THE PROCESS OF IMPRINTING

As a breeder of Tennessee Walking horses, I understood the significance of imprinting. A foal is born. After the mare has licked the newborn dry, I'd get in the stall and rub it all over, stick my fingers in its ears and mouth, pick up its legs, pick it up, put a halter on it and begin the leading process. This regimen, beginning at moments after birth, was repeated daily for 30 days. It is called imprinting. An **indelible mark is made in the foal's brain** that master is in control. Later, training and breaking becomes fairly easy, because the power of that full-grown horse has been brought under control by the imprinting of the master. The horse is made useful for racing, for showing or for pleasure riding.

*Is your involvement with God so intimate
that you are allowing Him to imprint you?
Are you observing and enjoying the benefits?*

Examine the lives of spiritual giants of the past, those who have made a great impact on society. All seriously engaged with a fairly standard list of disciplines for the spiritual life. Engagement was accomplished with intensity. "Not a few verses here and there, not one drop of water every five minutes to take a shower. But a full faucet of the Word at once and for a sufficiently lengthy time." (Willard)

159

The **disciplines of engagement:**
  <u>study, worship, celebration, service, prayer, fellow-ship, confession, and submission</u> are designed to immerse us ever more deeply into God's kingdom by developing new habits, kingdom habits.

On the other hand, **disciplines of abstinence**:
  <u>solitude, silence, fasting, frugality, purity, sacrifice and at times, waiting patiently for direction</u> from God are disciplines of abstinence and are **designed to weaken or break the power of the flesh.**

<u>Solitude and silence</u> are disciplines to block out the hustle and bustle of everyday living that obstructs our listening intimacy with The Father. Henri Nouwen, in <u>The Way of The Heart</u>, describes solitude:
  "It is the place of conversion, the place where the old self dies and the new self is born, the place where the emergence of the new man and the new woman occurs."

Nouwen elaborates, "**In solitude I get rid of my scaffolding: no friends to talk with, no telephone** calls to make, **no meetings** to attend, **no music** to entertain, **no books** to distract, **just me - naked, vulnerable, weak, sinful, deprived, broken - nothing**....We enter into solitude to meet our Lord and to be with Him and Him alone....Only in the context of grace can we face our sin; only in the place of healing do we dare show our wounds. **As we come to realize that it is not we who live, but Christ who lives in us, that He is our true self, we can slowly let our compulsions melt away and begin to experience the freedom of the children of God. And** then we can look back with a smile and realize that <u>we aren't even angry</u> or greedy any more."

Fasting was directed by Jesus in Matthew 6:16: _When you fast..._ Fasting is a discipline that weakens the power food can have over a person. The gnawing stomach reminds us to pray for the specific object of our fasting - be it an area of desired personal growth or for the salvation of another. Fasting reminds us of our dependence on God.

Living **frugally** and **sacrificially** lends greater opportunity to give more to God's work. Living frugally and giving of our selves sacrificially breaks the power of indulgence and greed in our lives. We break from a "society that marinates in its own incestuous self-interest." (Manning)

Desiring to live in **purity** breaks the power of the flesh that creeps in and entices us to live contrary to God's standards of holiness.

Waiting on God for direction is possibly one of the toughest things to do in the Christian life. We are performers. Os Hillman writes in Marketplace Meditations,

> "So often, when God places a call on one of His children, it requires a separation between the old life and the new life. There is a time of being away from the old in order to prepare the heart for what is coming. It can be a painful and difficult separation. Joseph was separated from his family. Jacob was sent to live with his uncle Laban. Moses was sent to the desert for 40 years. Paul to Arabia for three years."

Waiting on God.

Disciplines of abstinence break or weaken the power of the flesh.

Moving from the base of the growth triangle (Biblical world view and self-discipline) we shift to the apex:

Not by might nor by power but by my Spirit...

Holy Spirit Empowerment

What we've spoken of so far can be done

161

shallowly in our own power, or deeply in the power of the Holy Spirit. *Not by might nor by power but by my Spirit, says the Lord Almighty*. Zechariah 4: 6

The Holy Spirit is the third person of the trinity who possesses all God's attributes and is fully God. **He indwells all believers** from the moment they trust completely in the Lord. He is our advocate, comforter, teacher who equips us for powerful, spiritual living. As we surrender our lives to God, His Spirit works deeply in and through us.

Romans 8:10-13:

> *.... And if the Spirit of him who raised Jesus from the dead is living in you, he who raised Christ from the dead will also give life to your mortal bodies through his Spirit, who lives in you....*

How is this Spirit-filled life observed? Is it by being in church every Sunday? Is it following a list of do's and don'ts? Galatians 5:22-25 answers this question:

> *But the fruit of the Spirit is love, joy, peace, patience, kindness, goodness, faithfulness, gentleness and self-control. Against such things there is no law. Those who belong to Christ Jesus have crucified the sinful nature with its passions and desires. Since we live by the Spirit, let us keep in step with the Spirit."*

Holy Spirit observed by fruit, gifts and power

The Spirit-filled life, that life that is being empowered by the Holy Spirit, is not only observable by its **fruit** but also by **Spirit-given gifts**:

I Corinthians 12:4: *There are different kinds of gifts, but the same Spirit.* The rest of the chapter spells out the diverse gifts given by the Holy Spirit so that Christians work as a well-functioning body ministering to each other.

Fruit. Gifts. Now look with me at a third dimension: **power**. Acts 1:8:

162

> *But you will receive power when the Holy Spirit comes*
> *on you; and you will be my witnesses in Jerusalem, and*
> *in all Judea and Samaria, and to the ends of the earth.*

The Bible is filled with passages demonstrating God's empowerment.

But power is available **even now** for all believers: Ephesians 3:20:

> *Now to him who is able to do immeasurably more than*
> *all we ask or imagine, <u>according</u> <u>to his power that is</u>*
> *<u>at work within us,</u>*

So, a last reminder of the role of the Holy Spirit: I Corinthians 3:16:

> *Don't you know that you yourselves are God's temple*
> *and that <u>God's Spirit lives in you?</u>*

Our role is to surrender to Him and allow Him to live through us.

A total surrender to the Holy Spirit doesn't come naturally.
Relying on our natural abilities or even on God's
provisions of the past is too common a path we take.

The value of pain and failure!

The Holy Spirit works so subtlely behind the scenes that we often fail to realize His strength and involvement. **We need constant awareness of our** utter dependence on the Holy Spirit. This awareness usually comes through loss or failure of some sort. Though painful, loss and failure are needed for us to recognize need for the Holy Spirit's empowerment of our lives.

The Holy Spirit's major ministry is not the spectacular but the consistent infilling, cleansing, anointing, empowering, guiding and making fruitful our lives.

Our challenge is to recognize our consistent need for Him. As we Yield ourselves to Him, **He will work** fully and freely within us, maturing us into the godly persons we want to be. Yield yourself to Him and He will anoint and use you greatly. Ephesians 2:10 guarantees it:

> For **we are God's workmanship**, *created in Christ Jesus to do good works, which God prepared in advance for us to do.*

Self-discipline and developing a **Biblical worldview** are significant in personal growth, but of utmost importance is recognizing that a yielded vessel in God's hands is being "worked on" by Him, producing in us what we can't do through self-discipline or right thinking. It's not a legalistic religious standard that produces growth, but a simple living in the presence of God.

A Summary

As we conclude our venture in anger, dear reader, let's close with a summary statement. The Christian desiring growth that results in less unhealthy anger, learns that **maturity is not a formula but a walk**. **It is not a legalistic set of rules.**

> Maturity in Christ comes from taking what life delivers as allowed by the hand of God. Life at times will be painful or confusing. One with a **biblical world view** will process the pain with God and then focus on how God is using the situation for good. He will know that **deep character growth is a result of the process**.

Maturity in Christ also involves **discipline**.

- **Disciplines of abstinence** designed to weaken or break the power of the flesh.
- **Disciplines of engagement** immersing us ever more deeply in Christ-like habits that propel us into a *"character, falling short in nothing."*

The biblical world view and the thrust of discipline is not accomplished by relying on our own strength and wisdom but on the **power of the Holy Spirit.**

164

His subtle work within us stimulates our appetites for deeper intimacy with Christ, guides us into that divine romance and provides the empowerment to carry out the maturation process, the transformation we desire. **We provide the vessel. He provides the working power.**

As Bruce Wilkinson says: "You and I are always only one plea away from inexplicable, Spirit-enabled exploits. By his touch we can experience supernatural enthusiasm, boldness and power. Ask everyday for the Father's touch."

<u>**One of the greatest exploits of the Christian life is enjoying a diminishing unhealthy anger.**</u>

Scriptures:

James 1:2-4: <u>***Consider it pure joy***</u>, *my brothers,* <u>***whenever you face trials***</u> *of many kinds, because you know that the testing of your faith develops perseverance. Perseverance must finish its work so that you may be mature and complete, not lacking anything*

2 Peter 1:5-10   *For this very reason,* <u>***make every effort***</u> *to add to your faith goodness; and to goodness, knowledge; and to knowledge,* <u>***self-control***</u>*; and to self-control, perseverance; and to perseverance, godliness; and to godliness, brotherly kindness; and to brotherly kindness,   love ... For if you do these things, you will never fall.*

Not by might nor by power but <u>***by my Spirit***</u>*, says the Lord Almighty. Zechariah.4: 6*

But the fruit of the Spirit *is* <u>*love, joy, peace, patience, kindness, goodness, faithfulness, gentleness and self-control*</u> *Galatians 5:22-23*

Prayer:

Father, it is my desire to be a maturing Christian, one with less propensity to unhealthy anger. Show me now my responsibility in the growth process.

How can I learn a greater sense of Biblical world view?

_____

_____

_____

How do I need to increase my discipline of engagement?

_____

_____

_____

What area of my life needs a discipline of abstinence:

_____

_____

Am I seeking a more consistent infilling of and dependency on the Holy Spirit? _____

_____

The author is indebted to Dallas Willard with concepts and some material adapted from his book, Divine Conspiracy

Appendix one

Becoming a Member of The Family of God

John 3: 16-17 "For God so loved the world that he gave his one and only Son, that whoever believes in him shall not perish but have eternal life. For God did not send his Son into the world to condemn the world, but to save the world through him."

Jesus died for you and me. Believe in Him and receive eternal life. Believing one has one hundred dollars in the bank does no good until he acts upon the belief.

John 14: 6 Jesus answered, "I am the way and the truth and the life. No one comes to the Father except through me."

Jesus Christ is the only way.

John 1: 12 Yet to all who received him (Jesus), to those who believed in his name, he gave the right to become children of God.

By an act of your will, not feelings, you receive Christ. Ask Him to come into your life and take residence there.

Ephesians 2: 8-9 For it is by grace you have been saved, through faith— and this not from yourselves, it is the gift of God— not by works, so that no one can boast.

Living a good life does not get one to heaven. Receiving God's gift of salvation is your heavenly entrance fee.

Revelation 3:19b-20 So be earnest, and repent. Here I am! I stand at the door and knock. If anyone hears my voice and opens the door, I will come in and eat with him, and he with me.

If you've never opened the door of your life to allow Christ to enter, why not now? Receiving Christ involves turning to God from self, trusting Christ to come into our lives to forgive our sins and to make us what he wants us to be. It is not enough to give intellectual assent to his claims or to have an emotional experience. We must, by an act of our will, ask Jesus Christ to come into our lives, forgive us, and turn us around from a self-centered life to a God and others-centered life.

If you have not made the discovery of knowing Christ personally, may I invite you to receive Christ as your Savior and Lord now? Your attitude, not words, is what is important; but it may be helpful to prayer something like the following:

"Lord Jesus, thank you for loving me and dying for my sins. I need you. I now receive you as my Savior and Lord. I turn from my old life and expect a new growing life in you. Thank you for forgiving my sins and giving me life forever with you."

Saying these words did not give you the gift of salvation. But if your attitude is depicted by these words, then Christ is in you and wants to give you an abundant life.

Learn about this truth of salvation. Get to know God better. Time with God each day in study, prayer and meditation is very important. Christian bookstores have literature pertaining to Christian growth. The Gospel of John in the New Testament is an excellent place to begin study. Attendance at a Bible-believing church is important.

Knowing God better helps us know ourselves better and, in turn, helps us to see the resources we have in him to change those areas of our lives that need changing.

Appendix two

Biblical references to Anger and bitterness

Bitterness
Acts 8: 23 For I see that you are full of bitterness and captive to sin."

Eccl.7: 26 I find more bitter than death the woman who is a snare, whose heart is a trap and whose hands are chains. The man who pleases God will escape her, but the sinner she will ensnare.

James 3: 13-14 Who is wise and understanding among you? Let him show it by his good life, by deeds done in the humility that comes from wisdom. But if you harbor bitter envy and selfish ambition in your hearts, do not boast about it or deny the truth.

Hebrews 12: 15 See to it that no one misses the grace of God and that no bitter root grows up to cause trouble and defile many.

Anger
Ephesians 4: 31 Get rid of all bitterness, rage and anger, brawling and slander, along with every form of malice.

Colossians 3: 8 But now you must rid yourselves of all such things as these: anger, rage, malice, slander, and filthy language from your lips.

1 Tim.2: 8 I want men everywhere to lift up holy hands in prayer, without anger or disputing.

James 1: 19-20 My dear brothers, take note of this: Everyone should be quick to listen, slow to speak and slow to become angry, for man's anger does not bring about the righteous life that God desires.

Matthew 5:21-24 "You have heard that it was said to the people long ago, 'Do not murder, and anyone who murders will be subject to judgment.' But I tell you that anyone who is angry with his brother will be subject to judgment. Again, anyone who says to his brother, 'Raca, ' is answerable to the Sanhedrin. But anyone who says, 'You fool!' will be in danger of the fire of hell. "Therefore, if you are offering your gift at the altar and there remember that your brother has something against you, leave your gift there in front of the altar. First go and be reconciled to your brother; then come and offer your gift.